AT THAT TIME

Font and Table Series

The *Font and Table Series* offers pastoral perspectives on Christian baptism, confirmation and eucharist. Other titles in the series are:

Related and available through Liturgy Training Publications:

AT THAT TIME
CYCLES AND SEASONS IN THE LIFE OF A CHRISTIAN

Edited by James A. Wilde
With a Foreword by Mary Perkins Ryan

CONTRIBUTORS
John F. Baldovin
Ade Bethune
Andrew D. Ciferni
Lawrence S. Cunningham
Peter Mazar
Gertrud Mueller Nelson
Barbara O'Dea
Mark Searle
James A. Wilde

Liturgy Training Publications

All references to the Rite of Christian Initiation of Adults (RCIA)
are based on the text and the paragraph numbers of the 1988
edition © 1985, International Committee on English in the Liturgy;
© 1988, United States Catholic Conference.

"Fast Days" by Barbara O'Dea first appeared in *Catechumenate:
A Journal of Christian Initiation* (July 1988).

"Initiation and the Liturgical Year" by Mark Searle first appeared in
Catechumenate: A Journal of Christian Initiation (May 1987
and July 1987). It originated as a talk given at the Southwest Liturgical
Conference, Beaumont, Texas, January 1987. Used with permission of
Sister Virgil Kummer, OP, conference coordinator.

Liturgy Training Publications
1800 North Hermitage Avenue
Chicago IL 60622-1101
For all orders: 312/486-7008

Printed in the United States

ISBN 0-930467-87-6

Design: Jane Kremsreiter

Art: Ade Bethune

C ▪ O ▪ N ▪ T ▪ E ▪ N ▪ T ▪ S

■ FOREWORD

For catechumens, the newly baptized and all Christians who wish to deepen their participation in the liturgical, spiritual and social life of the church, the chapters of this book provide rich and varied material for information and reflection. To illustrate this, as the book's official first reader so to speak, I would like in this Foreword to offer some thoughts on the book's title, *At That Time*.

"At that time," of course, is the phrase that used to introduce each proclamation of gospel stories at Mass. There it reminded us that what we were about to hear was not some timeless myth but part of the good news of God's wondrous deeds for our salvation carried out at some definite time in the *past* and proclaimed to us *now* to influence our hope for the *future.*

In its liturgical celebrations, the church does much more than simply recall the past. What the Second Vatican Council's first fruit, the *Constitution on the Sacred Liturgy* (CSL), calls the "mysteries" of Christ's incarnation, life, death and glorification are sacramentally re-presented, made present to this time, our time. Therefore, at Easter we can truly say, "This is the day the Lord has made. Alleluia!" and on Christmas, "Today Christ is born!" At the same time we can also taste in anticipation the final fulfillment of God's saving work in "the life of the world to come."

The church brings past and future mysteriously into the present time. In order "to accomplish so great a work, Christ is always present to his church, particularly in her liturgical celebrations." By his power, he is truly present in the Mass in the persons of the ministers. He is truly present in the eucharist under the forms of bread and wine. He is truly present in his word, for it is he himself who speaks when the holy scriptures are read in the church. Finally, he is truly present in each faithful member of the church praying and singing together, because he promised, "Where two or three are gathered together in my name, there am I in the midst of them" (Matthew 18:20).

Christ is present to his church in so many ways not bound to time. He is "Christ yesterday and today, the beginning and the end, Alpha and Omega. All time belongs to him, and all the ages" (from the preparation of the paschal candle at the Easter Vigil).

So it is that when we take part in the liturgical life of the church, we can meet with Christ our Lord present in each member of the assembly. We can pray and offer ourselves to the Father "through him, with him and in him."

As the mysteries of God's love unfold in Christ throughout the church year, we can share his experiences and bring our own into their light. Therefore, in cooperation with the work of the Holy Spirit, day by day, week by week and year by year, we can allow ourselves to be formed as members of the body of Christ building itself up in love (see Ephesians 4:15–16).

For this to occur, we must take part in the public worship of the church with proper dispositions, with minds attuned to our voices and in complete cooperation with heavenly grace. If our participation is to be fruitful, we must be "fully aware of what [we] are doing in the rite, actively engaged in it and openly enriched by it" (CSL, 11).

That is not all. The cycles and seasons challenge us in other ways too (see CSL, 12). The spiritual life of church members is not limited to participation in public worship. We Christians are without doubt called to pray with others, but we are called also to pray privately to our God: "When you pray, go to your inner room, close the door and pray to your Father in secret. And your Father who sees in secret will reward you" (Matthew 6:6). Furthermore, according to St. Paul in 1 Thessalonians 5:17, we are invited to "pray without ceasing." We are always to carry around in our bodies the dying of Jesus, so that the life of the risen Lord Jesus Christ may be made manifest in us (see 2 Corinthians 4:10–11).

At That Time would not be complete if it failed to discuss the cycles and seasons of community building, world building. "Holding loyally to the gospel, enriched by its resources and joining forces with all who love and practice justice, the Christian must render an account of her or his time to God who judges all people" (*Pastoral Constitution on the Church in the Modern World, 93,* Second Vatican Council).

There is a time for public worship and private prayer, a time for commitment to justice and peace and a time of deep hunger for the fullness of the reign of God in this world. The pages of *At That Time: Cycles and Seasons in the Life of a Christian* should surely help readers cultivate these values and skills.

▪ *Mary Perkins Ryan*

■ CHRONOS AND KAIROS

What is time? A "cycle," says the person who lives close to
nature. "Like everything else, time is that which flows," said
Heraclitus. "A moved image of eternity," said Plato. "Measured motion," said Aristotle. "A continuum that lacks spatial
dimensions and in which events succeed one another from
past through present to future," says wordy *Webster's Ninth
New Collegiate Dictionary* (1988).

Stephen W. Hawking begins *A Brief History of Time:
From the Big Bang to Black Holes* (New York: Bantam, 1988)
with a story about a well-known scientist (probably Bertrand

Russell) who was once giving a public lecture on astronomy. He waxed long on current theories of the earth orbiting around the sun and the sun, in turn, orbiting around the center of a vast collection of stars called our galaxy. At the end of the lecture, a little old lady at the back of the room got up and said: "What you have told us is rubbish. The world is really a flat plate supported on the back of a giant tortoise." The scientist gave a condescending smile before replying, "What is the tortoise standing on?" "You're very clever, young man, very clever," said the old lady. "But it's turtles all the way down!"

Beginning with this picture of a universe as an infinite tower of tortoises, Hawking moves with ease through theories of deep space, distant galaxies, black holes and quarks. Drawing the layperson through antimatter and the "arrows of time," he reveals unsettling possibilities of time running backward when an expanding universe collapses, a universe with 11 dimensions, the theory of the "no-boundary" universe that may replace the big bang theory. He talks about a God who may be the prime mover in the creation of it all.

With care Hawking explains Galileo and Newton. With attention bordering on reverence he walks through Einstein's theory of relativity (concerning the extraordinarily vast) and this century's other great theory of quantum mechanics (concerning the extraordinarily small). Concluding, he explores the current great effort to combine the two into one quantum theory of gravity, the grand unified theory (GUT) that should answer all scientific questions left open thus far. Hawking, the young professor at Cambridge and, according to many, the most brilliant theoretical physicist since Einstein, sees this decisive discovery as close at hand.

But now we leave the world of dictionaries and science to enter the world of poetry, the world of metaphor and image. Now we turn away from the empirical world of accurate measurement to enter the world of meaning and life: the world that ties things together, the world of religion. Soon, too, the *super*GUT, which brings face-to-face that marvelous world of scientific discovery and that religious world of ultimate meaning, will appear on the horizon, and, as Bertrand Russell's little old lady may appropriately have challenged, after this long winter, "once again the voice of the turtle will be heard in the land" (Song of Songs 2:12).

At That Time: The Large Picture

For most human beings, by far the most ancient and still the most pervasive view of time is the cycle. From the perspective of the history of religions, the human observance of the cyclic rhythms of the day, lunar month, year, life span, century, millennium and aeon all spring from a religious attempt to please the gods by repeating or imitating their action in the creation of the world. (See Mircea Eliade, *The Myth of the Eternal Return*, New York: Harper and Row, 1954.)

Fertility rites, celebration of the new year, anniversaries of all kinds, purification rites such as baptisms, or the expulsion of demons or diseases or sins, all dancing, chanting-in a boatload of kumquats in Melanesia or the shrimp boats in Tampa, planting and harvest festivals, enthronement (or inauguration) ceremonies for new leaders, making designs in sand or concrete in the form of a mandala or the face of a god, birthday parties and thousands of other ritual events—all these originated or still are part of the human attempt to abolish the terror of history by gaining the favor of gods through repetition of the act of creation. Thus we return *in illo tempore* (at that time), *to start anew, with everything right this time.* Much in the Hebrew and Christian traditions reflects a cyclic view of time. All forms of millenarianism reflect this view. Much healing ritual reflects this view. Biblical or doctrinal fundamentalism most frequently reflects this desire to regenerate time. The myth of the eternal return is as common and persistent as the rising sun.

When through Israel the belief in one God above all other gods introjected itself into this prevalent cyclic view of time—this Lord God whose loving presence touched everyone—human beings finally had a way out, an escape. The Lord God revealed a new closeness to Israel by telling even the divine name to them. God said, "I AM WHO I AM. Say this to the people of Israel, I AM has sent me to you" (Exodus 3:14). Continuing the metaphor, the Lord God replaced the cycle with an arrow for those chosen ones, a line with a beginning and an end. From the first moment of Abraham's faith in God, there was liberation from history's terror and sin.

Chronos

Chronos is the Greek word for "time." From it we derive such American English words as "chronic," "chronicle," "chronograph," "chronology," "chronometer."

The Greek translation of the Hebrew Bible known as the Septuagint, undertaken from about 250 to 150 BCE, uses "chronos" for three or four different Hebrew words. Chronos translates "period of time" in Joshua 24:29, "a life span" in Isaiah 23:15 and "the time that eats away a garment" in Isaiah 51:8. It also translates the "time to prepare the way" in the Qumran *Scroll of the War of the Children of Light Against the Children of Darkness*, 9:19.

In Hebrew and Jewish writings, chronos, the opposite of the cycles described previously, translates words that view time as an arrow, having both a beginning and an end. Nor is chronos even the spiral: the Gnostic, Mary-Baker-Eddy or Jonathon-Livingston-Seagull "onward and upward" or, conversely, the Faustian whirlpool.

In the Christian Scriptures, written in Greek, chronos most frequently means "span of time" (see Gerhard Delling, *"chronos,"* in Gerhard Friedrich, *Theological Dictionary of the New Testament*, 9, Grand Rapids: Eerdmans, 1973, 581–93). Acts of the Apostles 1:21, Romans 7:1, 1 Corinthians 7:39, Galatians 4:1, for example, all carry this meaning. The span of time may be undetermined (Mark 2:19), or it may be fixed (Acts of the Apostles 7:23; 13:18). It may seem long (Acts of the Apostles 8:11; 14:3; 27:9) or short (John 7:33; 12:35). When it speaks generally of a maturing process (Acts of the Apostles 7:23), it denotes simply the maturing of a span of time, like 40 years, not maturing in the sense of growth to a higher state.

Chronos in the Christian Scriptures makes no basic statement about time in the formal sense (see Oscar Cullmann, *Christ and Time: The Primitive Christian Conception of Time and History*, Philadelphia: Westminster, 1950, 60; this classic is highly recommended to the advanced student of biblical interpretation). That is, chronos does not imply that time itself comes to an end. All that is meant is that the judgment of God will definitely occur and salvation will be decisively fulfilled as proclaimed. This is the meaning of *"After a long time* the master of those servants came and settled accounts with them" (Matthew 25:19) in the parable of the talents. This is also the meaning of "A man planted a vineyard, let it out to tenants and went into another country *for a long while"* (Luke 20:9), in the parable of the murderous tenants.

Frequently Paul and other writers influenced by him use chronos in an interesting way as the *long time before the NOW* when the gracious work of God in Jesus Christ is given to us already before eternal life. Romans 16:25–27 is an instance: "To God who is able to strengthen you according to my gospel and the preaching of Jesus Christ, according to the revelation of the mystery that was kept secret *for endless ages but is now* disclosed and through the prophets is made known to all nations, according to God's command, to bring about the obedience of faith—to the only wise God be glory for ever through Jesus Christ! Amen."

Generally, chronos is the span of time extending from creation to final judgment. In a metaphorical way it denotes duration between beginning and end.

Kairos

Kairos is the Greek word for a "decisive point in time," "opportune moment." According to *Webster's Third New International Dictionary*, kairos means "a time when conditions are right for the accomplishment of a crucial action."

In the Hebrew Bible more frequently it is God who seizes the kairos (Job 39:18, Numbers 23:23, Ecclesiastes 7:17). It denotes the "time of judgment" and the "last time" that God brings (Lamentations 1:21). Frequently it refers to the Day of the Lord at the end of the world (Ezekiel 22:3, 7:12; Genesis 6:13; Lamentations 4:18). Finally, God is boldly compared to kairos in Judges 13:23.

The people of God in the Hebrew Bible, like the author of Ecclesiastes, can see the direction of God in the series of kairoi through which God passes (Ecclesiastes 3:10–14). Usually the word carries positive implications, like "propitious hour" (1 Maccabees 12:1).

In the Christian Scriptures kairos usually means the "fateful and decisive point," with strong, though not always explicit, emphasis on the fact that it is ordained by God. There is a clear grasp of the rich, incalculable and gracious goodness of God in the gift of the kairos and of the judicial severity of its once-for-all demand. Thus Jerusalem did not recognize the unique kairos when Jesus came to save it (Luke 19:44), and there can be no second chance (see Gerhard Delling, *"kairos,"* in Gerhard Kittel, *Theological Dictionary of the New Testament*, 3, Grand Rapids: Eerdmans, 1965, 455–64).

According to Mark 1:15, the fact that this kairos of God's gift is now fully present is the first startling declaration of the primitive gospel proclamation of Jesus. The seriousness of decision is intensified. The more fully the transformation of the world is viewed, the more urgent is the demand of the kairos that recurs with every moment in the life of a Christian. Therefore, the Christian needs to recognize it and concretely fulfill the demand of the kairos (Romans 13:8–10). For now the Christian, born from above in the Spirit of Christ, is able to recognize it and fulfill its command (Galatians 6:10).

Kairoi, according to the Christian Scriptures, occur according to a schedule of development that God lays down. God gives each kairos its content; believers await each kairos with confident assurance. God ordains the kairos, whether it be the time of the manifestation of the word of God in Jesus (Titus 1:3), the proof (the word for proof here is "witness," "guarantee," "martyr") of divine love by Jesus in his crucifixion (1 Timothy 2:6) or the time of the epiphany of Christ (1 Timothy 6:15) and of the ensuing happiness of believers in the reign of God (Galatians 6:9).

Generally, kairos is the decisive moment for salvation, calling forth decision from human beings and judgment by God. The kairos par excellence is the passover of Jesus Christ from death on the cross to risen glory. The kairos par excellence for any individual in the community of Christ's disciples is similarly the moment of biological death and passover into the fullness of risen glory with Christ.

Kairoi in Human Life

It is easiest to speak of thousands of kairoi in the life of Jesus, of the church, of a nation or of any individual: thousands of deaths and resurrections; thousands of decisive moments; thousands of opportune times; thousands of crosses and resurrections; thousands of passovers, each one rooted in the mystery of God for salvation. It is appropriate, therefore, to view these thousands of kairoi as a dynamic series leading to full, eternal union with God. This is a history of salvation for each individual or for the whole human race. There is the big, universal story of salvation told to us in the Bible. And there are the individual stories, the stories of salvation that each of us tells for herself or himself: the Gospel according to Minnie, the Gospel according to Jake. All these stories are about kairoi, decisive moments of God's gifts and our response.

Infancy

An infant is by nature *self-centered*. He or she passes over from the cross of death to the glory of resurrection as birth takes place, as self-discipline, a dying, is imposed out of love for the mother or father or as new challenges for growth present themselves. How the infant copes with waiting or how she or he reflects a desire for more and more life may express clearly the way that kairoi elicit appropriate decisions. All of us have some infant inside of us.

Adolescence

The kairoi for the adolescent are *membership* and *law*. Teens meet these kairoi daily. How can I join society? What must I do to be a member in good standing? When faced with the kairos of church membership, will there be integrity or facade? Will the adolescent work hard enough to articulate a tradition's prayer practice or belief system or will corners be cut? When loyalties and trustworthiness are tested, will the adolescent come off the winner or the loser? In school, in the military, in courtship, in marriage, in citizenship, will the choices reflect infantile self-centeredness or will they reflect the budding responsibility of early adulthood?

Adolescents are already old enough to die and rise with Christ. St. Theresa of Lisieux, St. Maria Goretti and hundreds of saints in each junior or senior high school have proven it frequently. The cross and the resurrection consist most frequently in lending support to existing institutions or cultural mores or going against them.

Early Adulthood

Rationality is frequently the kairos of early adulthood. Early adulthood is about individuation, clarifying one's own values as opposed to those of others, including parents, peers, supposed authorities and the majority. Many people truly go through death to discover these values, but the result is a growth beyond anything previous.

One kairos through which many pass is the question, "In whom do I believe?" Another: "To what values am I committed?" Still another: "Where do I find the values that most convince *me?*" During God-given kairoi like these, frequently people take time out from church membership just to "sort things out," as they may say. Some find the presence of God, the ground of being, the horizon of existence more impressively on a hike, beach or golf course than they do in church. Unfortunately our churches do not encourage an integrative or growth-oriented response to this kairos because it may involve a considerable reduction in cash flow for the church.

Meaning for me is the kairos of early adulthood. Membership and laws no longer hold attraction; sports, science, creativity and insight, sometimes involving counseling, mind-altering drugs, advanced study or self-improvement techniques—all these are part of the early adult world. Chronological age, intelligence, education, background play only a small part in the graciousness or lack of it with which a person moves through this kairos.

Mature Adulthood

Image, symbol, community building, peacemaking and *other-centeredness* are the stuff of mature adulthood. "What return can I make for all that I have received?" That is the question in the heart and on the lips of the mature adult. "How can I surrender myself more for my service to others, to God who loves all, to everyone in the world with whom I am at one?"

As the infant draws all to herself or himself, the mature adult lets go of everything for the benefit of others. Frequently mature adults trade in psychiatric couches for spiritual directors. They live in a world of meaning drawn from symbol, from centeredness. Their power lies in the fact that they have found themselves and no longer need to grasp and pull at gratification or identity.

Depending on the way in which the kairos is given and received, the mature adult may end up moving back to the churches, any of the churches, not because he or she cares about membership or fear consequences but because that is where the people are who need community building, consolation and healing. Kairoi are great equalizers. Mature adults move beyond the church with the church to serve others. A mature Christian thrives on the eucharist as food enough for daily life, even heroism. Frequently apostolic works of peace and justice follow suit to the prayer for mature adults. They may live from the lectionary—the stories and words, the biblical images of God's love. The people in the stories and the words on their lips—these give daily life to the mature adult.

Discipline, related to Christ's obedience unto death on a cross, transforms the mature person by the grace of God so that she or he becomes the risen one, full of joy and wholeness. Responding with faith to the kairos gives the mature adult another drum to which to dance. The heroism of mature people sometimes looks foolish to the lesser of us. Readiness to die in response to the kairos, like Martin Luther King, Jr., Jesus, the apostles, Gandhi and many others, is the fruit of adult maturity.

Continuity

The healthy tension between chronos and kairos runs through the life of everyone. In their own way and from their own perspectives, the authors tell the story of the days, weeks, years and life spans of kairoi. The ordinary times and the special times rhythmically asserting, balancing and relaxing in their dance toward eternity—Ryan, Ciferni, O'Dea, Nelson, Mazar, Baldovin, Searle, Cunningham, Bethune, and Wilde. Stay with us, won't you?

▪ *James A. Wilde*

■ CHRISTIAN DAY

One of the most enduring myths that has come down to us from ancient Greece is that of Prometheus. Our unconscious still responds to this story of the hero who stole fire from the gods in order to bring it to humanity. I suspect that if we would take the time to reflect upon our power to create artificial light and heat we would also come in touch with the persistent power of the Prometheus story.

The Life of Day, the Death of Night

Without the power to make fire or to generate electricity we would be almost totally dependent upon the light and warmth that come to us from the sun. We are, however, a nation so accustomed to the almost universal availability of artificial light and power that we rarely advert to the extraordinary gift we have in our ability to control our environment, to extend our day, to make ourselves comfortable. A crisis of deprivation or an opportunity for leisure are frequently our principal moments of reflection upon these gifts that we usually take for granted.

Blackouts, brownouts or other power failures bring us face-to-face with the fragility of human-made environments. We stumble about in search of candles. We huddle around a fireplace or stove. We sit near windows where the first or last rays of the sun enable us to read. Camping out, however, introduces us to similar deprivation. The experience of it becomes an opportunity to be in closer touch with a world far less controlled by our switches and dials. During a power outage or on a long outing we frequently come to a new awareness of that basic rhythm of life that we call *day*.

No Meetings after Dark

The day as we experience it in the 20th century differs considerably from any previous human experience of the same 24-hour period. Before gaslights and Thomas Edison, human activity depended far more radically upon the rising and setting of the sun. Before a room could be flooded in light at the flick of a switch, men and women literally waited for the dawn so that they could get to the work of the day.

I never cease to wonder at the way early Christian authors speak about predawn cockcrow as though they were looking at a Seiko watch. They presume that their readers understand exactly what time they mean when they write about first cockcrow. It is obviously a time when the night is still dark but a time when fowl sensitivities alert duller human ones to the onset of dawn. Those who have slept on the farm know this. Contemporary city dwellers do not.

I suspect that one reason Augustine of Hippo was able to turn out so voluminous a corpus of theology was that an early fifth-century author could dictate by candle or lamplight and a secretary could take dictation by the same light. The clergy could not, however, call a meeting after dark unless they had the wax or oil resources of the very wealthy. Even then, one needed a platoon of guards to escort people safely through dark streets to and from the meeting.

The shape of the day in the 20th century is influenced far more by our need for sleep and meals than it is by the availability of natural light or by the narrow range of human social activities possible in the light of wax candles and oil lamps. When we endure a prolonged period without power or when we choose to be without power, we come close to the experience of the day that our ancestors had from the beginnings of human consciousness until the middle of the 19th century. What happens within us when we touch that ancient human experience? What happens within us when we rise early in order to drive to the top of a mountain or walk to the water to catch the first rays of the rising sun? Might we not make the same journey to be present to its setting? What emotions well up as we sit at the kitchen window watching the dawn's orange-pink light creep over the treetops? What does the heart feel when the mind becomes aware that we are turning on more and more lights while we wind up our deskwork or prepare dinner in the late afternoons of December and January?

Applauding the Sun

I've been told that people in Key West, Florida, head toward the shore each evening to watch the sun set. Evening after evening as the last bright orange solar sliver sets below the horizon, the silent onlookers burst into applause. Are they applauding the stunning performance of the day gone? Could they be assuring themselves that the sun will reappear for yet another spectacular show? Might they be giving themselves mutual supportive affirmation in the darkness that is now settling around them? The answer is yes! I've lived most of my life with Philadelphians who migrate across New Jersey each summer to get to the ocean. Friends and relatives, notoriously difficult to wake from slumber for school or work, display on vacation a remarkable capacity to rise in the dark in order to be on the beach when the sun begins to rise over the ocean. These are symbolic experiences. They stir the human heart. They stir so deeply that they hint at still deeper stirrings. What gives these events such power?

The rising and setting of the sun, the onset of day and night, dawn and dusk, the first rays of the sun and the lighting of evening fires and lamps are all connected with our ability to do the work that enables us to live.

They have to do with the leisure and rest we need to come back to work re-created. Ultimately the gift of the sun—completely outside our control—and our mastery of fire (electric and atomic power) determine our survival.

The realities of human survival are inevitably our most powerful symbols: touching one another, sharing food and drink. The more essential to survival a reality is, the more powerfully evocative is its symbol and the less able we are to explain how deeply it stirs the human heart and mind with affect and meaning. Nonetheless, I would like to suggest a few of *day's* meanings to show how Catholic Christians have employed its symbolic power to express their common faith in the death and rising of Jesus Christ as the root meaning of life.

Morning Promise, Evening Rest

How does the fresh morning speak to us? What does the dawn say? For early risers predawn is an incredibly quiet time: no phones, no doorbells, little if any traffic, uninterrupted quiet. Perhaps that is why the phone, the doorbell, the siren or loud movement in the house at this time speaks to us of grave emergency. Normally this is a time of promise. What does the new day hold? What do I eagerly expect? What do I fear will happen? How we greet the dawn depends so much on what is happening in our individual and social story on any particular day. The bride greets the dawn in a far different way than the woman anticipating a radical mastectomy. The groom's father might experience a bittersweet sense of completion that is far from the terror and anger in the heart of a father whose son will be arraigned the same day for assault. Less dramatically, the greeting of the day might be marked by a simple but open willingness to take what comes as it comes, a healthy sense of acceptance, an opening of the head, heart and hands to receive as gift the hours of light and what transpires within them.

What of the evening? What stirs within us as we realize that the sun's light is fading and that we need to turn on lights to continue our work? No longer for us the ending of the workday with the setting of the sun. Evening for us is more an extended end-of-the-third-quarter break to breathe deeply after the accomplishments of the day and to prepare for the works that we will carry on after dark—works possible only because we have received incredible light. If we dare to pause just before we turn on the lights, we may come in touch with a previously unconscious sense of fear that comes upon us with the dark. We are all afraid of the dark. We know it on a moonless night when we are lost on a country road without a map. We know it when we are camping out in the mountains. Unfortunately we might even know it in the parish parking lot or while walking home from our city parish center after a meeting that ran until 11:00 PM.

The power to control light has been given into our hands, and many of us accept the gift with an unconscious arrogance of invincibility. We are not subject to the natural flow of day until the lights go out, and we realize that not only are we out of batteries but that we have never learned how to build a fire! It is not my purpose to suggest that our power to control light is "unnatural" or bad. This power is a gift, and it has made us less than totally dependent upon nature's daily cycle. It is my purpose to suggest that we would do well to be in touch with the stirrings of the human heart at the beginning and end of the day, at the beginning and end of the night. I submit that it is only when we become conscious of morning's mixed sense of promise and anxiety—our own and others'—and evening's ambiguous sense of rest after labor combined with an uneasy feeling about the possible dangers of the dark, that we will be in a position to cherish the gift extended to us in the Catholic church's ancient tradition of morning and evening prayer.

Life Gives Birth to Ritual

Human rituals seem to emerge most spontaneously at the hinge moments of life: birth, beginning of physical or social adulthood, marriage, child-birth, serious illness, death. It comes as no surprise then that men and women have prayed at dawn and dusk, at the hinge moments of the day symbolized by the rising of the sun and the lighting of lamps. This religious instinct was taken up by Israel and by the followers of Jesus. Whether in the instruction we learned on our parents' laps—"Be sure to say your prayers"—or in the lessons of liturgical history of the solemn celebration of Lauds and Vespers in cathedral and monastery, Catholic Christians have seen their day shaped by morning and evening prayer. The prayer takes up the stirrings of the heart into the prayer of Jesus. What we suffer and what we glorify is joined to the death and rising of Jesus and becomes part of his sacrifice of praise.

These critical moments of prayer are first and foremost acts of praise to God arising from thankful hearts. We give thanks for the light of the sun, the Light of the Sun of Justice who visits us with healing. Morning Prayer is, moreover, an act of dedication. What the day promises, we direct to the honor and glory of the Giver of Light. As the light fades, we illumine our spaces of prayer and common life while we sing our praise of Jesus Christ, the Light who never fades, whose brightness is not subject to the alternation of days and nights. Our evening prayer gives thanks for what God has been able to work in us throughout the daylight hours. Our sense of inadequate response to God's gifts is expressed in prayers of repentance. We pray for protection throughout the coming darkness. We look forward in hope to a new day.

Daily Prayer after Thomas Edison

Because our experience of the day has changed so radically in the last century, we should not be surprised that the shape and experience of daily prayer has also been modified. People who have been enabled to work far into the hours of darkness should not be surprised that they do not have the enthusiasm for early Morning Prayer exhibited in the writings of fourth- and fifth-century Christian writers who retired to bed at a much earlier hour. On the other hand, the hectic nature of our workdays and the frequent use of the lunch hour as a time given to re-creative activity can help account for the popularity of midday prayer services of one form or another. Hinge moments in human life continue to be shaped and celebrated in ritual prayer. If for millennia the lighting of lamps to extend the day has been an occasion for giving thanks for our ability to make light, prayer immediately before retiring for the night has been one of the most popular and traditional times of prayer among Christians. Night Prayer (Compline) sung in dark monastery chapels or family bedside prayers express our fear of the dark and our desire for the protection of the God who gives every gift of light. Because the moment is so full of meaning, the prayer retains its power. In virtually all societies while most of the members sleep, someone keeps watch, someone keeps vigil. A society called to vigilance for the coming of the Day of the Lord could not but call some of its members to express in the prayer of vigils the whole community's longing for the bridegroom who will come when we least expect him. Every night of the year many monastic women and men come to prayer while most of us are deep in our dreams. At least once a year all the church keeps Vigil as it brings to birth from the Easter font new children of God. Dawn and dusk, high noon and bedtime, the middle of the night—how much of our story as human family is told in reference to these times! How much promise and disappointment, how much fear and deliverance come to awareness as we move through these hinge times in the flow of night and day! Resurrection discovered at dawn, crucifixion at noon, death and burial at eventide, deliverance in the night—how much of our story as a Christian community is told in reference to the times of our praying!

Prometheus: Christos-Helios

One of the first depictions of Christ in art known to us comes from a Roman mausoleum mosaic discovered in the excavations under the Vatican basilica. In a ceiling of gold a lush grapevine turns and curls. At its center is the sun chariot and the four horses of Apollo (Helios to the Greeks). The driver is a young beardless white-robed man whose head stands out against the background of the sun. In the midst of the sunburst, however, is the cross. This is Christos-Helios, Christ the Sun of Justice. This is the Christ we greet when at the lamplighting hour we sing "Jesus Christ is the Light of the world. A Light no darkness can extinguish." This is the true and everlasting Prometheus who brought us fire not stolen but rightfully his own, who died not in punishment for the fire given but to show us how the fire could consume for the life of the world. The myth lives on but is transformed.

We, too, are transformed as day by day we allow ourselves to contemplate the reality of human life shaped by the rising and setting of the sun. A people believing in the "fleshtaking" of God's Word knows that every movement of the heart triggered by the passing of light and darkness is a movement to be celebrated in prayer that makes our life and suffering, our pain and rising, one with him who brought fire to the earth.

▪ *Andrew D. Ciferni*

■ FESTIVAL DAYS

Shout for joy before the Lord, you who are righteous;
  praise comes well from the upright.
Give thanks to the Lord on the harp;
  sing psalms to the Lord with the ten-stringed lute;
Sing to the Lord God a new song:
  strike up with all your art and shout in triumph.
  — *Psalm 33:1–3*

Thank God for festival days! Thank God for days of songs and "shouts of triumph," for days to live out and act out our assent to the whole of creation. Since the dawn of consciousness, humankind has known the need to take time out. Work, however rewarding and necessary, is not the highest end in life. And the feast day is necessary to civilization and culture as much as industry ever was. Today, perhaps more than ever.

When we lose the right balance of that truth, when we lose our reason for feasting, we are a sorry society. A field that is planted and harvested without ever lying fallow or being renewed with dung becomes leeched of its richness. A people that blurs its days one into the other and loses its festal days to a work ethic has lost its meaning and its connection to the Holy Other. As the people of God keep the feast, so will the feast keep and sustain the people.

Looking thoughtfully at our society's ability to celebrate, it would seem that our weekdays, our Sundays, our feasts and holidays, our vacations, our sabbatical leaves, even our retirement years, while paradigms of the kingdom and steeped in promise, too often dissipate into a season of panic or despair because we still have not learned to embrace the art of living. Perhaps our society would have us believe that only the gross national product will bring a people salvation. Have we forgotten that what we yearn for is to be "re-souled" by a touch with the transcendent?

A day surrounded by regulations *forbidding* work and a day that invites us to worship to rejoice in God, Sunday is our challenge to be fully human. During the week we *co-create* with God. With our talents, our trade, our time, we support ourselves and, if we are true to our baptismal commitment, we sustain each other. We are asked to carry into our daily lives the wonderful works of liberation, healing, straightening, enabling, alleviating, transforming, that the Lord worked on the Sabbath.

On the Lord's Days (Sundays) and on festival days, we are given the chance to *recreate* and "play with God on equal footing." We do this for the sheer joy of it and for the very health of our humanness. Plato said it delightfully:

> The gods, taking pity on humankind, born to work, laid down the succession of recurring feasts to restore them from fatigue and gave them the Muses, Apollo and Dionysus as companions in their feasts so that, nourishing themselves in festive companionship with the gods, they should again stand upright and erect.

In Sirach, too, we are told that the festival day is a day of special divine intervention:

Why is any day better than another when all the daylight in the year is from the sun? By the Lord God's decision they are distinguished, and the Creator hallows, and some of them God makes ordinary days.
— *Sirach 33:7–9*

Sunday is the physical and spiritual renewal of all humankind as each individual creates the "life of the world to come." On that day and on the feast days of the year, we celebrate as though all that we have been working toward has already been accomplished. We affirm that things are "very good."

The Festival Days of the Church Year: A Structure for Wholeness

The church as a mother always centers on the cycles of our human development and nourishes us through rite and symbol, through the caring and patient repetition of feast and fast. As John Baldovin will point out in his chapter on the Christian year, the celebrations of the church year mark our own cycles and seasons. Over and over, the feasts invite us to engage, see, feel, touch, experience, grow strong and, finally, to be transformed. Like a mother, she cares about our birthing, marrying, failures and reconciliations, our dying and our rising again. When we celebrate the feasts of the church year with symbol and story and sacrament, the experiences that make up our daily lives are affirmed and made holy.

The traditions and rich heritage that the celebrations of the church year offer connect us to our ancient roots, to all who went before us and to those who will come after us. Celebrating together binds us together with a common symbolic form, a unique identity and a long tradition. Through rites and ceremonies, we find our place in the cosmos. When we celebrate through the structure of the church, we actually have the forms we need to become whole again, after losing that integrity through sin. We are given back a meaning for our days and for our common human experience, after losing meaning and true human exchange in our fall from grace.

The Nobility of Nature

It is always a temptation for us to believe that the everyday world and the sacred, the ordinary and the extraordinary, do not meet. That perceived schism prevents us from experiencing healing and wholeness. In fact, we cannot find our religious nature outside the setting of our human experience. The flesh taking of the spirit, the incarnation, is a mystery made new in our daily efforts to be human.

Rites and symbolic actions, celebrations and liturgies are meant to heal that rift. They help interpret serious human experiences like loneliness and community, successes and failures, births and deaths. They encircle the transitional points in our lives with celebration, those occasions when we take the risk of moving another step forward into awareness and transformation. They act out our hopes for the reign of God and our belief in its goodness.

When we feel too small, too insignificant, too inadequate to approach the Holy Other directly, we use the elements of nature that are within our reach. Nature and the things of this earth allow us to approach the Untouchable through what we *can* touch and understand. The elements used in liturgy and celebration, though simple and familiar, become icons of divine presence. More often than not they are the same elements, objects and experiences that sustained us as long as history can remember. In ritual and celebration, we encounter the transcendent in what is wonderfully familiar: in bread and wine, in fire and ashes, in earth, water and oil, in fast and feast, in pain and joy, in mind and body.

Create and Discover

To celebrate and be healed through the grace of our Christian heritage requires our rediscovery of the themes that the recurring feasts of the church calendar offer us. To these we apply our creative imagination—finding the bridge between our personal experiences and the whole inheritance of grace and sacramentality that is ours as members of Christ's body.

Celebration and liturgy are enhanced when we are sensitive to the grace-filled realities of experiences that already fill our days. The religious experiences that wait for us, incarnate in the human condition, will come to life for us. If we cannot be swept off our feet by the vision of God in a meal shared at home, how can the bread and wine of eucharist be a mystery for us?

If we want our festival days to be neither boring nor obsessive, we need to rediscover the rites and folk customs that lie buried in our heritage. New and fresh approaches to what is old and primal in human expression can emerge from our increased understanding of human nature. The sciences of psychology, anthropology and sociology can illuminate and breathe new life into our Christian feasts. We need to know our hunger at its deepest place—what is basic and primal to human expression and need. We need to know what our society offers us and what it denies us. In what ways does our society offer and deny us a healthy religious expression.

Advent and Christmastime

Waiting and preparing for Christmas during the season of Advent, for instance, is not so much an imposition of penance—even though it may be difficult to swim against our cultural tide of celebrating Christmas during Advent rather than at Christmas—as it is an opportunity simply to wait, to become spiritually pregnant, a condition from which our dominant cultural values hold we must be freed. Someplace very deep in us, we already know the value of waiting and "gestating" as necessary to anything of value. Christmas is richer when we have engaged in the experience of preparation and patient, happy anticipation. Furthermore, all the places in our daily experience, where waiting, gestating, hoping and preparing are needed in order to be human, become sanctified for our having engaged seriously in the rites of the season.

Festal and seasonal liturgies afford us the chance to *do something,* no matter how simple. In doing something, we once again allow the earthly process to carry God's hidden grace. A Native American said: "We do not believe our religion. We dance it." Advent wreaths and Christmas trees, Easter eggs and birthday candles, maypoles, wind socks, festal clothes, special foods, dances, songs, colors, cheers, tears—all of this is our human effort to put out the stuff through which the Spirit can breathe life, grace and meaning into our days. None of it is too humble. In fact, its ordinariness is what makes it worthy. All of this is as ancient as human existence. All of it needs to be renewed, remembered and kept worthy.

Weak Calendars and Strong Calendars

The parish calendar closely resembles the church calendar. There is one difference, however. Like the church calendar, the parish calendar moves back and forth between the mysteries and the body of believers. Unlike the church calendar, in a parish, first there is an assembly. Then, as extensions from that assembly there is the household and the greater community.

Community building is a natural result of involvement in what heals and builds us all. We should be careful, then, not to weaken the church calendar by scheduling bingo on Holy Thursday—yes, it happened last year—or bake sales during Lent instead of on Shrove Tuesday (Mardi Gras, the Tuesday before Ash Wednesday). Why should not the solemnity of the Assumption occasion a community picnic among the fields and trees and grasses where we can celebrate the holiness and fruitfulness of mother earth? The urgent issues of peace and justice find their foundation in God's revealed word, the lectionary. Even national holidays such as Independence Day, Labor Day and Thanksgiving, along with the appropriate lectionary selections, give impetus and renewed purpose to our commitment to justice and peace. If we observe these holidays fully and faithfully, they can become organic, center points of our worldview and mission.

Finally, if our celebration does what it sets out to do, through its richness and our involvement, it can knit up the gap between heaven and earth. We will be set back into life, discovering the symbols and vehicles of transformation in all the ordinary things of our lives: a word chosen with care, a meal shared with friends, a touch, a smell, a sight, a sound—all ordinary things become extraordinary when, bursting with the infusion of the Spirit, they are suddenly perceived as holy and "very good."

The Festivities of Carnival: An Example

Easter is of course the highest and most joyful feast of the year. Its joyful celebration lasts 50 days without interruption. All the other feasts of the year point toward Easter. Every Sunday or Lord's Day echoes it. Lent prepares us for it. In fact the final purifying weeks before Easter for both new and old Christians are founded on the disciplines of prayer, fasting and almsgiving.

Lenten Hunger. During Lent we are asked to consider what we hunger for. We live out the time of Lent not to replace the mysteries of dying and rising but to intensify those mysteries in our heart. We are asked to engage our death and the painful dismemberments we must undergo in order to become whole again. Misunderstandings, losses and separations, loneliness and longing, failure, illness, death, all the fears we know deep down—all cast shadows across our days. But we know we cannot come to the light unless we are willing to enter the darkness. Lent is engaging the "dark night of the soul."

The Art of Passing Over. In the Three Great Days, the Paschal Triduum, our disciplines are heightened, and finally during the Vigil the rites act out our drowning. Plunged into water, we are pulled up as newborns, wet and gasping. We are reborn and whole again! Death is defeated!

Eastertime Festival. Named, anointed, initiated, feasted with eucharist, sung to—the rite unfolds into the most magnificent victory celebration of the year. So great and holy is this festival, so passionate and primal, that human nature has coughed up a kind of antidote. Every time things get very splendid, we find a shadow preceding or following it. All Saints' Day is preceded by the revelry of Halloween. Ashes precede the baptismal waters and fragrant oils of Easter. How else could we possibly approach the wonder of Easter with its resurrection joy except by beginning with death?

The Pilgrimage from Carnival to Lent. The reverse is true, too: How else could we approach lenten order and death than by going first in the opposite direction with Mardi Gras—that is, by "living it up?" Carnival precedes learning how to die by allowing us to live for a time in a compensatory period of recklessness and fantasy. It is that dreamlike place offered by tradition that celebrates with wild pageantry the dark, unknown powers of the soul.

Though our example is the movement from Mardi Gras to Ash Wednesday, the same festival principles touch the whole church calendar: every feast, each solemnity, all seasons. See the fuller development of these elements of celebration in my book, *To Dance with God: Family Ritual and Community Celebration* (New York: Paulist Press, 1986, 45–55). Each season and festival is treated in detail: Advent (59–95), Christmastime, including Epiphany (96–127), Carnival and Lent (128–62), the Triduum (162–82), Eastertime (182–95), the Assumption (196–219), harvesttime (220–41).

Civilized societies in every part of history and in every part of the world recognized this need to return from time to time to chaos. That is because for every step we take into the light of grace and consciousness, we also have to remember and honor what is still dark and messy, disorganized and iconoclastic, just the other side of consciousness. Carnival lets loose for a time our negative, irrational and unacceptable selves and, by engaging and remembering what is dark and steamy in our condition, lends us a warning: The darkness of human beings, if projected outside of our personal responsibility rather than accepted and integrated into the personality, is capable of horrible, even global, disasters. Through this ritual action we are also confronted with the fragile beauty of our human condition. Carnival is the ritual hint at the goodness that lies behind our longing for that "re-souling" touch of the Transcendent.

What is unacceptable and unruly in our human condition insists on being admitted into our awareness. Wherever one virtue has been developed to excess, the impulse is to compensate and bring about the opposite. And in turn, where great concentration and introspection is in order, we want to let go and be oppositional. Like dumping out all the drawers on the floor before we begin ordering and sorting things, we see everything messed up and turned upside down. Carnival offers this sort of compensation to the ordering of Lent.

The history of carnival itself has gone through pendulum swings in the course of time. We hear of extraordinary excesses (for example, New Year's Eve revelry lasting well into Lent) and playful irreverence (for example, the monks' night off for Halloween). Where the church was once tolerant, even understanding, she then stepped in and condemned almost everything. This left the festival so tame and anemic as to allow no genuine release for the tumbling, untamed impulses of humanity. Mardi Gras celebrations in New Orleans and many cities of Europe have little to do with religious observance. They are not followed by the prayer, fasting, almsgiving and death of Lent.

Good or Whole? If we dig back into ancient wisdom, the basic issue becomes clear. In the quotation from Plato cited previously, festival days are humankind's opportunity to celebrate together with the Muses and Apollo and Dionysus as our companions for the nourishment of all that makes us fully human. Isn't it just like a cautious, law-abiding parent for the church to suppress our companionship with Dionysus and approve only of our friendship with Apollo? *Asking us to be good is asking us to be incomplete. But asking us to be whole is inviting us to be holy.* For both attitudes that these gods represent—creative tumult and law and order—are valid aspects in life. They may be complementary, but together they offer balance. Neither side is better nor more valuable than the other. Rather, both sides enrich our lives when they are brought into recognition and integration.

The festivities of carnival deal with opposites, with compensation and balance. The figures and exaggerated shapes that parade the streets during carnival in big cities indicate just that: Men dress as women, and women dress as men. The poor dress as the rich, and the rich dress as the poor. Those who feel inferior tease and reveal the true stature of those who act as their superiors. Clowns and jesters, true to their tradition, unmask the powerful and return them to us for what lies behind their masks and motives.

Carnival, for all its appearance of mayhem and its dabbling in danger, is the ritual expression of all that wells up from the forgotten level of our souls and that on every other day of the year we would rather not face. On this day it receives consideration and celebration. In fact, the dark aspects and the shadow side of our existence are recognized as having a deep and rich gift to offer if we can now face it squarely and honor it freely. We laugh more, we cry more, we play more, we eat more.

We express feelings that are normally repressed or forgotten because they have no form to contain them. Our forgotten self is affirmed as valuable despite everything. It holds the missing pieces that would make us whole.

Carnival as a Parish Celebration

Just before Lent then, we can plan and celebrate a family or community carnival remembering that carnival (literally, "Farewell, flesh") or Mardi Gras (literally, "Fat Tuesday") works only insofar as people also want to take their lenten observance seriously. To have the first without the latter is to be false about the celebration. Furthermore, as with so many festival days, we may take over for ourselves the traditions that preceding generations have handed us. We may not cling to the external appearances alone. What really matters is not simply the preservation and conservation of a quaint celebration. Celebration also requires our creative infusion of insight so that the content of the festival continues to make a vital impact on the celebrants.

In preparation for the feast, each person looks inside, perhaps with the aid of dreams, and brings up for consideration those aspects of the self that one might wish to keep buried. We unmask our carefully constructed *personas* and remask with the best representation of our hidden self. "By masking, one unmasks a supernatural source."

Dressing as the Shadow

To discover or engage our shadow, buried at the bottom of our souls, we need only to look to those neighbors, those relatives, those TV personalities, those public figures, the nightmare characters who people our dreams, the heros, whoever arouse in us the strongest feelings. The feelings might be negative: disgust, fear, disdain, avoidance, longing. The feelings may also be positive: admiration, adulation, worship. That person or type who calls forth intense feelings is our shadow, our hidden and forgotten self.

Body as Friend. This year, I will have to dress like a Dallas cheerleader. It is much easier to dismiss such a woman as an "airhead," shallow, giddy, flirty. Certainly she has no depth. And then I begin to think about it. She *is* rather like me. How embarrassing! She leads a celebration and values the expression of joy and festivity—just the qualities that I like to think are my realm. She knows how to "shout for joy," to "sing a new song," to "strike up with all her art and shout in triumph!" Furthermore, she is fit. I have been in my head so much these days that I have neglected my body. I've put on weight and hide myself in an oversized shirt while I write my papers. She can be all legs and arms and smiles. She can jump and tumble with abandon because she likes her body. She eats right and exercises. So, these must be some of the things that I have not wanted to address. These, indeed, are valuable issues that fit right in with the disciplines of Lent. Fasting is done for the good of the whole person: body, soul, image, heart, spirit. What am I going to do for the good of my whole self, including my body, because I care, because I believe that the mystery of the incarnation and the resurrection of the body makes the body worthy of care?

My friend tells me he absolutely hates disorder and messiness. He dislikes illogical thinking, poorly written articles, junky garages, disorderly closets, slovenly dressers, people who drop things and ask for instructions twice, people who are late for appointments and everyone who eats junk food. His list is long and is reeled off to me with genuine passion. The passion tells me we are close to something real. Perhaps he will have to dress as a bagman this year, I suggest. But he objects immediately, declaring his great contempt for costumes and dressing up. His trim, groomed, preppy look is just fine, and, indeed, he begins to itch all over and scratch at the very thought of a bagman. But slowly, with a combination of courage and distaste, he begins to imagine the life of the bagman. And what possible kernel of riches could the bagman possibly have to offer him? A look of vulnerability sweeps over his face and he says softly: "The bagman is not driven by a schedule. He can be spontaneous. I could learn to be more spontaneous. I probably would see and feel much more than my driven style of living affords me." My friend begins to make some simple resolutions for incorporating the bagman into his lenten exercise.

Put on Fresh Clothes, the New Person, Christ. People arrive at the parish hall, dressed or masked as their hidden selves. There is a great mix of excitement, humor and vulnerability in the air. People are explaining their costumes to one another. All this dressing up will have further meaning as Lent turns into Easter. The church has used the concept of special dress at moments of regained innocence and fresh beginnings: the white garment of the newly baptized, the white garment of first eucharist, the white garment of the bride and even the white funeral pall over the coffin. They all carry the same overtone of new beginnings or a transcending of one's fallen state.

When we need to reform, when the call is for penance and atonement, we are asked to "put on sackcloth and ashes," a custom from a distant, pre-Christian past (originally Akkadian and Egyptian, but see Isaiah 58:5, Jeremiah 6:26, Ezekiel 27:30–31, Daniel 9:3). At Easter, however, we are called by Paul to "put on the new person," "to put on Christ." From that emerged the folk custom of Easter bonnet or Easter outfit. But that is a wholly different kind of dressing up that comes at the end of our 40 days of preparation and the loving integration of our shadow selves. For now we will live out these characters that we have unearthed from the bottom of our souls. We incorporate them into the games and dances, the singing and the feasting, all evening long.

Because carnival means "Farewell, flesh," "Farewell, meat," "Farewell, all rich things" that we forgo until the Easter feast, we have one last sampling of everyone's best desserts. The traditional dishes that turned up during carnival actually used up the rich ingredients that were being cleared out of temptation's way before the great fast.

Burying the Alleluia. After the feasting, after the last games and dances, we sing our final Alleluia and we sing it in rounds. Then we bury it in a deep chest. The Alleluia that we bury is first lettered on a long scroll and decorated with spring flowers by all the participants. We will not hear or use this expression of greatest joy until it is sung again during the Easter night. Then we settle down. We remove some of our silliness and gather for community night prayer. Drawing the revelry to a close, we face into tomorrow's Ash Wednesday. We offer one another a sign of peace and best wishes for a holy and fruitful Lent.

With that, we begin a great silence that will last through tomorrow morning. Everything is cleaned up, and everybody moves about collecting belongings, but no one speaks a word.

Tonight I have danced with the bagman. Tonight I have danced with a general. I have danced with clowns and cowboys. I have danced with the president and an elephant. I have danced with a cheerleader, with Apollo, with Dionysus. Tonight I have danced with God.

The assembly disperses and returns home in silence to wash off the paint, to make faces ready for tomorrow's sign of ashes. Our celebration helped us, and we feel ready, now, for the discipline of Lent.

▪ *Gertrud Mueller Nelson*

■ FAST DAYS

My interest in fasting began with a conversation on the role of fasting in the catechumenate. Somewhere inside, we all knew that witness is more important than words. Yet in this significant area of Christian life, what we as ministers seemed to be saying to our newest members was: "Don't do as I do; do as I say." That posed a more basic question: Does/should fasting have a place in the life of Christians or not?

In grappling with the question, we recalled that the goal of Christian initiation of adults is conversion and faith resulting in personal commitment to a gospel way of life and integration into the ecclesial community. That raised other questions. Is fasting related only to the dimension of *personal* conversion and commitment? If not, how can we speak of fasting for *those in the process of initiation* unless the *initiating body* itself values and practices it?

Approaching the question of fasting out of that context led me to explore:

— fasting in the church

— fasting and conversion

— fasting in the life of a Christian.

Fasting in the Church

It seems safe to say that, corporately, American Catholics at the present stage of postconciliar church life place no clear value on fasting. While it is true that several church documents encouraging fasting have appeared over the past 15 years, most of the faithful are unacquainted with them. Pastoral leaders also seem unaware of the existence of such encouragement for fasting or unconvinced that this pertains to the lives of contemporary believers. Perhaps at this point in the process of renewal, it is time to reexamine the gospel tradition on fasting in order to discern its message for contemporary believers.

Gospel Tradition. There are a number of gospel passages that relate Jesus' teaching and fasting: Jesus fasts in the desert before beginning his public ministry (Matthew 4:1–4); he teaches about fasting in the Sermon on the Mount (Matthew 6:16–18); he refers to the current Jewish practice in the story of the pharisee and the publican (Luke 18:9–14).

The text that most clearly states Jesus' position on the subject is the Matthean passage:

> When you fast do not put on a gloomy look as the hypocrites do; they pull long faces to let all know that they are fasting. I tell you solemnly, they have had their reward. But when you fast, put oil on your head and wash your face so that no one will know you are fasting except your Father who sees all that is done in secret; and your Father who sees all that is done in secret will reward you.
> — *Matthew 6:16–18*

It is important to note that in this section of the Sermon on the Mount, which might be called "Rules of Asceticism for the Community of

Believers," fasting is presented as part of the trilogy: almsgiving, prayer, fasting (Matthew 6:1–18). All are given equal importance and parallel treatment in the passage. All are integral to a gospel way of life. (See Joseph F. Wimmer, "Almsgiving, Prayer and Fasting," in *Fasting in the New Testament*, New York: Paulist Press, 1982.)

Fasting is assumed: "*When* you fast . . ." This is followed by some cautions: Don't act like hypocrites; don't put on long faces. Then Jesus presents his positive teaching on the subject: When you fast, let it be with no external signs; let it be for the Father who knows all that is done in secret. It is for this kind of fasting that Jesus promises a reward. For Jesus' disciples, not only the act of fasting but also the motive that inspires it is important. Fasting is for the Lord. It is to be an act of worship, of submission to the Father.

Early Church. Manuals of church discipline and, later, writings of the church Fathers continued the evangelical tradition. They encouraged fasting in conjunction with prayer and almsgiving. Christian writers presented fasting as part of the normal rhythm of Christian life. A second-century manual of church order, *The Teachings of the Twelve Apostles*, more commonly known as the *Didache*, states: "Your fasts must not be identical with the hypocrites. They fast on Mondays and Thursdays, but you should fast on Wednesdays and Fridays." Christians were obviously taking care to distinguish themselves from Jews. How lamentable that in the very act of preserving the weekly fasts of the Jewish tradition, the *Didache* author would also use Matthew's bitter term "hypocrites."

The same document encouraged fasting as a means of converting the hearts of persecutors. To Matthew's text, "Bless those who curse you; pray for your enemies" (Matthew 5:44), it adds, "Fast for those who persecute you."

In the same century, the author of *Clement's Second Letter to the Corinthians* envisions fasting as leading to repentance and good conscience. Fasting prepares the heart and mind for *metanoia*, change of heart.

Even at this early stage in church life, the practice of fasting was already linked to the sacrament of baptism in what later came to be known as the paschal fast. The *Didache* teaches:

> Before the baptism, moreover, the one who baptizes and the one being baptized must fast and any others who can. And you must tell the one being baptized to fast for one or two days beforehand.

Later in the same century a similar practice of the church in Rome is noted in *The First Apology of Justin:*

> How we dedicated ourselves to God when we were made new through Christ I will explain. . . . Those who are persuaded and believe that the things we say and teach are true, and promise that they can live accordingly, are instructed to pray and beseech God *with fasting* for the remission of their past sins while *we pray and fast along with them.* Then they are brought where there is water and are reborn.

Note that in both churches it is not only the candidates for baptism who are to fast but also members of the community.

Conclusions. Many insights of importance to today's Christians can be gleaned from this overview of fasting in early church discipline:

— Fasting must not be seen in isolation, but as one part of the gospel triptych: almsgiving, prayer, fasting.
— Motivation is the key. Fasting must be for purifying the heart and drawing closer to God.
— Fasting was understood to be integral to a Christian way of life.
— Fasting was considered part of the ordinary rhythm of Christian living.
— Early in Christian tradition, fasting on the part of the candidates and of the church was linked closely to baptism.

The teachings on fasting in the early church are important because the understanding of the role of fasting in Christian life later became confused. When fasting was separated from this evangelical perspective, prescriptions and distinctions made Christian fasting into something narrow and trivial. The legalistic approach of the article on fasting in the *New Catholic Encyclopedia* (1967) illustrates how far we had wandered from the gospel spirit. It entertains such trivia as whether nondigestible matter (paper, fingernails, tobacco) break the fast. Small wonder that contemporary Catholics find little meaning in fasting. Christian asceticism has yet to be explored in the postconciliar church.

Fasting and Conversion

Having glimpsed the role of fasting in the life of the early Christian church, let us now focus on the connection between fasting and conversion and the challenge it presents to contemporary Christians.

We have seen that for Jesus it was not a question of whether or not his disciples should fast. Rather, it was a question of *why* and *how* they should fast. To become his disciple, one must deny self, take up one's cross and follow him. But what does that mean for Christians today?

As Christians it is our vocation to make the death-resurrection of the Lord the pattern of our lives. We proclaim it every Sunday as *the* mystery of our faith. We baptize new members into Christ's death and resurrection each year at the Easter Vigil.

If catechumens and neophytes have gradually been initiated into the mystery of our faith and understand it as the very dynamic of Christian living, they know, like Paul, that they too must "die daily." They come to see that conversion is a gradual process of turning away from selfishness, sin and destructive inclinations, as one turns toward Jesus Christ manifest in the word, the church and in the world.

For Christians who have seriously undertaken this way of life, catechumens, neophytes and veteran faithful alike, it soon becomes evident that to live this conversion, self-discipline is needed. While the call comes from God, a faith-filled response is possible only with consistent effort. Conversion without asceticism is an illusion.

In a wonderful book entitled *Fasting Rediscovered,* Thomas Ryan defines asceticism as "any conscious practice that helps us move from a self-centered to a God-centered life." There is no *metanoia,* no change of heart without it. To reach out to new life and growth in Christ, one must let go of the evil, the egoism, the clutter in one's own life. That is where fasting comes in.

Christian fasting is a response to the Spirit's action drawing people to open their hearts to God's love. Through fasting the body is kept in healthy control thus disposing the one fasting to greater awareness of the call of God in the circumstances of life. Through fasting the body is cleansed, the mind and heart cleared. Fasting leads people to simplify their lives, to discipline their advertising-induced needs and to transcend self to the point of embracing all Christ came to save. Such fasting leads to a growing experience of union with God and to deep peace.

Such fasting has a communal dimension. Strong in the preconciliar church, the witness of mutual support through fasting together has disappeared in the contemporary church. Fortunately, the seeds of renewal have been sown in several significant documents calling Christians as a body to fast.

In the 1966 pastoral statement abrogating the previous laws of fast and abstinence, the bishops of the United States highlighted the fact that the need for penance and self-discipline remains. True to early Christian tradition, they asked for voluntary abstinence on all Fridays of the year, complemented by Christian service. (See also *Paenitemini*, Apostolic Constitution of Pope Paul VI on Christian penance, February 1966.)

In response to the crisis of world hunger, the American bishops issued another significant invitation. They appealed to Catholics to fast at least two days a week, especially during Advent and Lent. Further, they restored the connection between fasting and almsgiving by asking that diocesan programs of worship, fasting and abstinence be set up and that "funds from such fasting . . . be directed toward ministering to the needs of others." (See "A Pastoral Plan for the Food Crisis," November 1974.)

More recently, in their pastoral letter *The Challenge of Peace: God's Promise and Our Response* (May 1983), the bishops again urged Catholics in the United States to witness to our need and desire for peace through corporate fasting on Fridays. This fast is to be "accompanied by works of charity and service toward our neighbors."

Through these statements the bishops call Catholic Christians to conversion. Their teachings about fasting are reminiscent of early church observance. They invite believers to a corporate expression of faith in the Lord and to an increased awareness of the needs of others through prayer and almsgiving.

Fasting in the Life of a Christian

Christian conversion consists in a radical transformation of life in response to God's call. Although it is often possible to pinpoint a turning point/conversion in one's life, we know that conversion is not only an *event* but a *process*. "Repent and believe the good news" signals not only the beginnings of Christian discipleship but its underlying pattern. Growth in faith is the way we follow Christ. Fasting, because it halts the dissipation of energies and creates perspective, can be a powerful stimulus to the conversion process. It serves as a connecting link between prayer (which draws us to an increasing awareness of God's presence in our lives) and almsgiving (which moves us to concerned response to the needs of others).

Fasting becomes an external manifestation of conversion within. Like Jesus in the desert, the one who fasts gives physical expression to belief that

God is more important than food, riches, power (Luke 4:1–13). Fasting becomes symbolic of turning away from all that weighs us down, all that inhibits our surrender to God. The very experience of physical hunger can trigger awareness of the many hungers in our lives: for forgiveness, for meaning in life, for peace, for community, for God's word, for justice in the world. Such fasting, when accompanied by a turning toward God in prayer and toward neighbor in service, witnesses to the fact that we no longer are centered on self but have found our center in Christ and in the gospel that renders the reign of God present on earth.

What Are Some of the Rhythms of Fasting? Tradition, church teaching, the rhythms of one's journey of faith and of the liturgical year are important considerations in discerning when one might fast.

Early Christians recognized the need for fasting as part of the ordinary rhythm of Christian life. They associated the practice with Friday, the day of the Lord's crucifixion. In memory of that event and in the spirit of the renewed consciousness of the contemporary church, might not Catholics fast on Fridays? Through regular observance of Fridays as days of fast, we will learn experientially the personal value of fasting and how to integrate asceticism into the rhythm of our lives.

Turning points on one's faith journey are obvious moments for fasting. On their journey, every follower of Christ faces moments of decision. Fasting at these moments makes us conscious of dependence on God. Fasting during a retreat, much as fasting during Lent or on the great vigils of the church year, disposes body and spirit to draw deeply from the meaning of these moments. When other members of the parish community pledge themselves to fast with us, fasting can spark common motivation to live the gospel.

As we Christians grow in commitment to the reign of God in the world, we grow also in awareness of areas of resistance to God in our lives. At such times, a sense of physical emptiness increases the desire to allow God to fill us.

Finally, the church year provides many occasions for personal and communal fasting. The Advent call to prepare the way of the Lord challenges Christians to reform their lives in order to make present the reign of God (Matthew 3:1–2). Lent, the church's annual retreat, calls the people of God to follow Jesus into the desert to fast and pray. The paschal fast on Good Friday and Holy Saturday prepares the body and spirit for the baptismal covenant of Easter. In addition, vigils before Pentecost, Assumption and other major feasts are invitations to prayer and fasting to prepare hearts to be open to the light of Christ.

Who Should Fast? Who Shouldn't Fast? An important consideration on the question of fasting is: Who should fast? A clue from early church tradition indicates that members of the community fasted with the catechumens. Today, might not the faithful of the community willingly fast with catechumens at appropriate times throughout the church year? (One caution: One should not expect catechumens to fast simply because they are catechumens. The nature of Christian fasting as a response to God's call must be respected.)

The invitation to fast should be issued to all members of the Christian community. Preparation of the parish community for the rites of initiation as well as the seasons of Advent and Lent provide opportunities for homilists and adult educators to reexamine the tradition and explore the meaning of fasting. The encouragement to fast and the opportunity to share reflections on the meaning and experience of fasting provide a catalyst for deeper reflection and conversion on the part of all who respond to the invitation. Mutual support in fasting is a powerful encouragement to grow in healthy self-discipline.

How Do You Start Fasting? Before you start fasting, consider these preliminary steps:
— Read the statements by the American bishops mentioned previously as well as other contemporary works on fasting and discuss with someone else, perhaps a spiritual companion, what these statements mean to you and what you are going to do about it.
— Go ahead and try it and then reflect on the experience.
— Seek out persons in the parish who have rediscovered the role of fasting in their own lives and listen to their experiences.
— Consider with them the prayer-fasting-almsgiving connection in Matthew's gospel.
— Ask questions regarding motivation for fasting: Why fast? How is this a prayer? For whom is this fast? What are you asking of the Lord for yourself or for people for whom you fast?
— Be conscious of almsgiving possibilities: Who needs the money or time set free by your fast?

Needless to say, that final question leads to extensive exploration of what it means for Christians to be stewards of creation and faithful disciples of the way traced by the Lord in the Sermon on the Mount.

Once the motivation for fasting has been considered, do not neglect the practical aspects:

— Begin slowly, perhaps first abstaining from a single meal, then a supper to supper fast.

— Drink fluids: water, fruit or raw vegetable juices so that the fast may be cleansing to body, mind and heart.

— During brief fasts one can carry out normal daily activities. Persons with particular health problems should not fast without medical advice.

— Have a light meal following a fast. This allows the body to adjust. Moreover, it avoids a fast/binge rhythm that undermines the purpose of fasting.

Conclusion

Often it is the newcomers among us who raise old and basic questions. This exploration of the tradition of fasting was sparked by a sense, perhaps a subconscious collective Christian memory, of the importance of fasting at key points during the process in the catechumens' growth in conversion and faith. It led to a rediscovery that the practice of fasting is deeply rooted in our Christian tradition. Fasting is integral to the rhythm of the life of the individual Christian as well as to the rhythm of feasts and seasons in the church year. Those Catholics sensitized to the call to reexamine the tradition of fasting will be challenged by deeper hungers that only the bread of word and sacrament and the growing consciousness of the presence of the Spirit in their lives can fill.

Barbara O'Dea

◼ THE SANCTORAL CYCLE

Modernity has had an enormous impact on the way we organize our time. Not until the latter half of the last century did the English language develop the word *weekend,* and the Romance languages still do not have their own word for it. The notion of a weekend was only possible when large numbers of urban people began to think of their times in terms of weeks instead of days. Agricultural societies think of daily chores and seasonal occupation. We tend to think of blue Monday and "Thank God it's Friday." The notion of the Sabbath is reduced now to mall stores not opening until noon on Sundays. The late morning Protestant worship hour as the main service is a lingering relic of times when people had to get necessary chores done and still make it to town for services.

A Changing Picture

Given such temporal shifts in the way we organize time, it is not surprising that the old cycle of honoring the saints with special feasts (the so-called *sanctoral cycle* of the liturgy) now exists in the popular imagination only in the relics of folkways: heart bedecked greeting cards on Saint Valentine's Day and green beer on March 17 to honor Saint Patrick. Particular cities (San Francisco) or dioceses (San Antonio) or religious congregations and their affiliated institutions may honor saints, but by and large, the old festivals of the saints do not loom large in the life of the average Catholic. It is the rare Catholic today who would celebrate a name day in honor of a patron saint; that custom has been totally replaced by the birthday celebration.

The church was not unaware of this shift. Both the Second Vatican Council and, more precisely, a 1969 statement of Pope Paul VI trimmed the calendar of saints in order to refocus the life of the church on the preeminent celebration of the Sunday liturgy. This reform pruned out of the calendar an overburdened canon of obscure, semilegendary and overinflated saints whose lives, meritorious in their own right, were of little significance for the universal church. The calendar committee self-consciously tried to introduce saints into the calendar who reflected the geographical diversity of the church. Nonetheless, only Catholic trivia buffs recognize many of the names in the revised calendar.

Do Saints Mean Anything to People Today?

The more compelling question is, of course, whether the calendar of saints has any significance at all to the worshiping community or whether, because their position is already in place, the saints ought to be simply invoked in the eucharistic prayer of each liturgy as a recognition of their place in the whole church and let it go at that. That question touches an even more basic one: What place do the saints have in the prayer life of the church and how can that place be recognized for what it is and for what enrichment it supplies to the community of the faithful at worship?

Although the word "saint" in the New Testament meant the members of the believing community (frequently St. Paul addresses the "saints" of a particular church in his greetings), historically the more specialized meaning of a saint as an extraordinary person in the church has its roots in the period of the Roman persecutions. From the late third century on believers began to commemorate the death days (called *natalitiae*, birthdays) of those who died under persecution. These celebrations were at their most fervent when held at or near the places of their burial. With the end of the persecutions, these celebrations had a profound impact both on the developing liturgy and the shape of sacred architecture. The saints were not only models to be imitated but were considered powerful intercessors before God. Their tombs were believed to be a locus of divine power. Early in church history saints were associated with miracles and prodigies. Recent scholarship on the rise of the cult of the saints has emphasized how important this devotion was in the history of Christianity both East and West.

After the period of the persecutions, more saints were added to the calendar of observance as writers began to emphasize the "white" martyrdom of the ascetics, monks and missionaries who were thought as worthy as the "red" martyrs who had shed their blood. The right to honor these saints was usually determined by the local church, but with the centralization of the church, this became a papal privilege until, in the late twelfth century, the right to canonize (that is, to put a name of a person on the list of saints or *canon*) was reserved exclusively to the Vatican.

The historical development of the devotion to saints in general and their liturgical commemoration in particular is an enormously complex subject that has not only historical challenges connected with it but social, political and folkloric elements as well. There are added elements of complexity such as the tension between the saint seen as miracle worker (for example, St. Jude as the patron of lost causes) or as model (for example, St. Francis of Assisi) and the tendency of the bureaucratic process of canonization to favor those who have the best access to the process. It is not surprising that one has a better chance of being named to the canon of saints if one belongs to a religious order of men or women with a motherhouse in Rome and the personnel, connections and, God save us, funds to push the cause with the Roman authorities.

Notwithstanding these historical and bureaucratic issues, saints are an important part of the Catholic tradition and their reality points to some deep theological truths and to some important pastoral opportunities. In the remaining pages of this essay I would like to focus on two points: the theological significance of the saints in the Catholic tradition and some suggestions for a pastoral strategy to integrate a theology of saints into the liturgical life of the church.

Theological Significance of the Saints

In the context of the liturgical celebration of the saints, either through their feast days or their daily invocation in the eucharistic canon, we are reminded that the church sees itself not merely as extended in time and space but as an eschatological community that has ties to the church that is already in Christ. The celebration of the saints, in short, is a concrete manifestation of the communion of saints and a sign of the hope that we possess for an ultimate life in Christ. In that sense, the invocation of the saints has an intimate connection with our remembrance of all who have gone before us and now "sleep the sleep of peace." We join our prayers with them as a single community of praise and worship. That is the deepest meaning of All Saints Day when we honor those who are canonized—not a single community who now make up the heavenly church.

Secondly, as the *Dogmatic Constitution on the Church* of the Second Vatican Council makes clear, the saints are those who have become true "images of Christ" for us. Another way of saying it: The saints serve to function as an example in our own pilgrimage of Christian conversion. Furthermore, the saints do that in one of two ways. Some saints demonstrate the continuing vitality of the tradition. Thus, a Mother Teresa of Calcutta would be doing the same thing were she transported back in time a thousand years. Her sanctity is rooted in the perennial evangelical imperative of finding Christ in the poor. Other saints emerge in the church to show us new insights into the gospel and new ways of living it out. Now that we have successfully enshrined them in stained glass it is difficult to realize how radical a Francis of Assisi or a Teresa of Avila looked to their contemporaries. A close understanding of saints in their own times provides clues about the fecundity of the gospel as it is played out in real lives. In that sense, as some contemporary writers are beginning to realize, the lives of our saints are a rich resource for theological reflection and for the doing of narrative theology.

Closely allied to the notion of the saint as paradigm is the prophetic role of the saint in the pursuit of the fullness of Christian living. The saints are, above all, *serious* people. What distinguishes saints from do-gooders is that saints do not suffer burnout. Their very lives are a judgment on how far we have to go and to what extent the gospel makes demands upon us. Martyrdom, for example, is not simply a romantic story of sighing maidens awaiting the lions' attack in the Colosseum. Contemporary martyrs have been on the front pages of newspapers. The contemporary iconography of the saints does not consist in the sword or the wheel of St. Catherine or the gridiron of St. Lawrence. Our symbols of martyrdom are the electrode, the bullet or the violation of the human body and mind through sexual humiliation, violence and death. That has happened to our contemporaries in Central and Latin America, in the gulags of the East and in the jail basements of Africa. Such lives not only judge our complacency but witness to the ultimate demands of the gospel. Martyrs, in short, are of tremendous value to Christianity because they underscore that side of the gospel that is in tension with the pretensions of the world.

Pastoral Suggestions for the Reintegration of Saints into Liturgy

However rich the hagiographic (writings about saints) tradition may be for the deepening of spirituality, it may be objected that this does not easily translate into a significant resource for the revitalization of the liturgical sanctoral cycle. I accept that objection on its face because I see no plausible way in which our calendar will refocus itself on the turning seasons of saints days and saints festivals. Indeed, I think that the 1969 statement of Paul VI did not go far enough. One could envision a single great feast of the Blessed Virgin, another for the Apostles and all the saints, and some days to be chosen *ad libitum* for the needs of particular churches. The plain fact of the matter is that the current calendar is peripheral in the life of worship and is likely to remain so. While it may not be a question of urgency, the whole issue of the sanctoral cycle needs some profound rethinking.

Nonetheless, it does seem possible to utilize the resources of our tradition of the saints in a serious way. Here are some particular suggestions:

(1) Some regular catechesis would be useful to explicate the reasons why Mary and the apostles and saints are invoked in the daily liturgy. Such a catechesis could explore themes such as those we have mentioned previously. Recent writings on the saints (see the books cited at the end of the chapter) give us the confidence to think that such a catechesis can be constructed with theological depth.

(2) It may be that special annual events in the parish (like the annual carnival or autumn parish dinner) coincide with a saint's day that would include some special tribute to a saint in conjunction with the festival and its liturgy. That may appear, at first glance, as a trivial suggestion, but it would be a start in helping to flesh out catechesis with liturgical praxis.

(3) It does not seem improbable to imagine special days of celebration that would allow a worshiping community to develop a significant theme and use that day to recall the great figures of our common Christian heritage. Why would a parish not set aside a "Peace Sunday" on an annual basis in which, as part of the liturgy, we call on great peacemakers (from Francis to Gandhi) to be witnesses to our desire for genuine peace? Such a day might fall on the Sunday closest to the anniversary of Hiroshima. An alternative is to commemorate all contemporary martyrs on a "Justice Sunday" in which people like Edith Stein, Oscar Romero, the four women martyrs of El Salvador (Maura Clarke, Ita Ford, Dorothy Kazel and Jean Donovan), Martin Luther King, Jr., and Dorothy Day could be honored in the context of the liturgy. Parishes that focus on other tasks of social justice (the celebration of life; the sensitization of people about hunger) could use the tradition of the saints to make concrete such concerns.

(4) All Saints Day might be revised as a day in which we honor the "hiddenness" of sanctity by a focus on all the unsung saints who have lived among us. Every Catholic knows truly authentic (albeit uncanonized) saints: people whose love and fidelity encouraged us or inspired us in our lives. We could ask parishioners to write out short paragraphs about those people to be read in tandem with a brief homily. Names are not always important: Everyone will recognize the types. Such a practice could be just as usefully employed on All Souls Day when such evocations take on special meaning.

(5) Historically, saints were linked with particular localities. Parishes might wish to remember in a special way, at well-attended feasts like Christmas or Easter, past pastors, religious or lay people who were particularly influential in the life of a parish or a town. At the Easter Vigil, for instance, it might be well to recall earlier priests who baptized previous generations. Such commemorations help enlarge the sense of tradition and continuity. Such practices also help remove the saints from their proverbial pedestals and provide a clearer understanding of saints as part of the larger community.

(6) In line with the previous suggestion we might begin to develop a local "litany of the saints" to be composed by segments of the parish to highlight those who have most shaped the community in its spiritual development. Why can there not be such litanies (they need not be endless in their listing) for use by a catechumenate group or the parish school or the various groups in the parish?

In whatever other creative ways people wish to celebrate the saints, they should do so with certain basic principles in mind: that such celebrations should foster our sense of unity in faith and our conviction about the eschatological dimensions of church life. We should especially honor those saints who help us grow in the life of Christ by teaching us about the power of the gospel. We must remind ourselves that the saints are not only those who exist on an official list (canon) or who have been consecrated in plaster of paris or mosaics. The saints are part of the pilgrim People of God who in their lives have sustained and taught us here and who now join us in the praise of God in anticipation of our own arrival in the heavenly Jerusalem that is Christ.

A final note. Despite the decline of liturgical interest in the saints in recent centuries, there has been an enormous increase in the scholarly and pastoral attention to the tradition of saints. It might be worthwhile knowing some titles of books in English that have been recently published. John Delaney's *Dictionary of Saints* (Doubleday, 1980) and Robert Hugh Farmer's *The Oxford Dictionary of Saints* (Oxford, 1978) are valuable compilations on canonized saints in the church. Peter Brown's *The Cult of the Saints* (University of Chicago, 1980) is a scholarly and insightful study of saints from the medieval period through 1700. Benedicta Ward's *Miracles and the Medieval Mind* (University of Pennsylvania, 1982) is a fascinating monograph on the cult of the saints and their shrines in the Middle Ages.

The anthology of essays compiled by Stephen Wilson, *Saints and Their Cults* (Cambridge University Press, 1983), is doubly valuable for its exhaustive bibliography. John Stratton Hawley's collection of essays (by many hands) *Saints and Virtues* (University of California, 1987) is helpful because of its attention to the place of saints in various world religions.

William Thompson's *Fire and Light: The Saints and Theology* (Paulist, 1987) is an attempt to utilize the saints as a resource for the doing of theology. Lawrence S. Cunningham's *The Meaning of Saints* (Harper and Row, 1980) is an attempt to recover the significance of saints in the Roman Catholic tradition. There is a brief but suggestive essay by Kevin Donovan, "The Sanctoral" in *The Study of Liturgy*, edited by Cheslyn Jones *et al.* (Oxford, 1983), while Notre Dame University's Center for Pastoral Liturgy devoted an issue of *Assembly* (November 1981) to saints in the liturgy.

■ *Lawrence S. Cunningham*

■ CHRISTIAN WEEK

Imagine being without clocks or calendars. Imagine having to start from scratch a system for dividing up time. Just using your own two eyes, you would be able to distinguish days, months, seasons and years—but not weeks.

You could divide time into days by observing sunrises or sunsets. (Our method of beginning new days at midnight wouldn't be very practical. Without a clock, how could you tell when it was midnight?)

You could divide time into months, although these would not be our 28-, 29-, 30- or 31-day periods. Instead, these months would be the time—about 29½ days—from new moon to new moon or from full moon to full moon. To measure these "months" you would have to watch the moon night after night going through its phases. In fact, that's the ancient meaning of the word month, from "moonth."

You could divide time into seasons in several ways. You could keep track of the changing weather or the migration of birds or the relative length of day and night. You could take note of what's coming into flower or fruit or what is passing into decay. Maybe these "seasons" wouldn't be the four we're used to, but with a little imagination you could invent as many seasons as you like, such as "the season of falling leaves," or "the season in which daytime lengthens" or "the season in which the barley gets harvested."

You could measure years by noticing when particular seasons recur. The year could begin and end, say, in the season the barley is harvested. If you gauged years this way, the length of such years would vary a bit depending on the weather.

You could be very precise about the year by observing the stars. As the earth revolves around the sun, the stars in the night sky keep shifting bit by bit toward the west. For example, the same stars that are high in the sky after sunset in autumn are low in the west after sunset in winter. Those stars appear low in the east a half year later after sunset in summer. You could mark the beginning of the year on the first day that a particular star—let's say the brightest star in the sky—appears low in the east just before sunrise.

All these periods of time, discovered with a good pair of eyes, are ways that people have kept track of time. Many of the world's religions—Jews, Christians and Muslims among them—have a preference for using the sun and the moon and the stars to "mark the fixed times, the days and the years" (Genesis 1:14). We seem to want our religious time dished up as naturally as possible.

Weeks

What about weeks? Is it possible to discover the week by observing the sky? It is not. True, the seven-day week is *almost* the period between each phase of the moon, say, between the new moon and the first quarter, or between the first quarter and the full moon. But if you judged by the phases of the moon, within only a few weeks everything would be out of sync.

It seems that giving a period of seven days and nights its own name is both ancient and yet strangely independent of any natural phenomenon. Unlike the day or month or season or year, the week is a human invention, discernible only to creatures who can count. It cannot be read in the heavens. The week can only exist if human beings count the days one by one, and then go back to the beginning after each count of seven.

The week gets much of its meaning from being so uniquely human:

> "That ye may know that I am the Lord who sanctifies you" (Exodus 31:13), the Holy One, blessed be he, said unto Moses, "I have prepared a precious crown in my treasure house, and its name is Week, and within it is a jewel that far outshines all others, and it's name is Sabbath. I wish to make of it a present to Israel. Go now and make it known to them."
> — *Babylonian Talmud*

Our scriptures tell us that the week is a unique gift from God. All the while God was fashioning creation, God was also fashioning the week a day at a time. While all creatures abide by days and seasons and years, only humans—and those creatures who work for humans—are able to observe the week, to order days toward a day of rest, the one day in seven that has been given for joy and delight.

> Between me and the Israelites it is to be an everlasting token; for in six days God made the heavens and the earth, but on the seventh day God rested at ease.
> — *Exodus 31:17*

A couple thousand years ago, the Romans conquered the Jews and decided that the Jewish seven-day week with one day for rest was a useful way to organize time. So they legislated the seven-day week throughout the Roman world. Judaism may have been the birthplace of the week, but the Romans brought it into universal use and gave the days names for some of their gods, the gods who wander around the heavens: Sun Day, Moon Day, Mars Day and so on.

Tinkering with Time

Since then, several nations, especially those cursed with dictators (who often appear to be amazingly efficient about getting things done), have experimented with other sorts of weeks. For example, after the French revolution someone got the bright idea that if the decimal system was good enough for money, it was good enough for time, so the ten-day week was instituted in the empire. It was a flop.

Tampering with the way we keep time is perilous. Just listen to the gripes that surface every time we need to change clocks to accommodate daylight saving time. Listen carefully to the way some complaints are worded. Some people think that we're actually adjusting the sun, not just our clocks. It may be a comic revelation of the profound belief that most people have that only God is the keeper of time.

Christians did their own tinkering with time, conservatively and carefully, and their success at reshaping time was in proportion to their respect for the natural cycles of sunrise and sunset, the passing of the seasons, the changing lengths of days, the rhythm of sowing and reaping. All these have become part of Christian life because we believe that they are epiphanies of God's reign. They are signs, and if they are interpreted in the wisdom of the Spirit, they are signs that point toward the Creator.

When Christians turned their attention to the week, with only one large exception they adopted in whole the Jewish week. In the tradition of the church, the last day of the week is still called the sabbath, in church Latin, "sabbatum." The second through the sixth days of the week are called, in the Jewish manner, "second day," "third day," and so on.

The church has never adopted the Roman names for the days of the week, though many of these Roman names came to be used in ordinary speech. The Romance languages use the Roman names for the second to the sixth days of the week. German- and English-speaking people named days of the week after a few of the Roman gods and a few of the Norse gods.

Our society and culture are not controlled by or often even conscious of the way the church keeps time. Those days are gone.

At Vatican II the Roman Catholic bishops acknowledged even the possibility of living with some kind of a "world calendar" whose months and years might be divided quite differently from our present system. But on one question of time they said the church could never compromise our calendar: The seven-day week is not altered or tampered with by any "uncounted" day. The succession of sevens—unbroken in Judaism and in Christian churches—is not something in our power to alter.

Sunday

Only on the first day of the week did the church choose to invent a name different than the Jewish name. The Jews call the day after the sabbath the "first day" of the week. Christians call it "The Lord's Day."

The "Day of the Lord" is a title straight from the mouths of the Jewish prophets. See Amos 5:18–20, Joel 2:1–2, Isaiah 13:9–10, Zephaniah 1:14–16. It meant something like Doom's Day or Judgment Day (not exactly a day to plan a Sunday picnic). "The Lord's Day" is a title also found in Christian scriptures, especially among Christians expecting Doom's Day any minute (Revelation 1:10, 2 Peter 3:12). In this sense, "Lord's Day" meant the day of the great epiphany, the coming of God to right all wrongs and to establish the reign of glory in heaven and peace on earth.

The Christian Lord's Day took on other meanings from the first day of the week. That's the day creation began, when God said, "Let there be light." The Lord's Day is a day of beginnings, a day of light separated from darkness.

A Day of Worship

The early Christians did not identify the sabbath rest with the Lord's Day, as later generations eventually did. In their society Saturdays usually were sabbathlike, a day free from work even among the non-Jews. But Sundays were workdays, so the Christians met after work for the evening meal to pore over the scriptures and to break bread and share the cup with praise and thanksgiving.

Sunday became a day of worship. Unlike the sabbath, which is dedicated to rest, Sunday is a day of special *liturgy*, a word with roots in the words "laity" (people) and "energy" (work). Liturgy means "the work of the people." After the seventh day, the day of rest, the first day of the week is the first day of the workweek, and the work to which we dedicate ourselves— our true liturgy—is our life's work in serving the Lord. And Sunday is the day of baptism, when we remember and seek to live up to our initiation into the passover mystery of Christ's death, rest and resurrection.

From the beginning of our Christian history, the Lord's Day has been the day to gather for a special kind of liturgy, the eucharist.

> By a tradition handed down from the apostles and having its origin from the very day of Christ's resurrection, the church celebrates the paschal mystery every eighth day, which with good reason bears the name of the Lord's Day or Sunday. For on this day Christ's faithful must gather together so that, by hearing the word of God and taking part in the eucharist, they may call to mind the passion, the resurrection and the glorification of the Lord Jesus and

may thank God, who "has begotten them again into a living hope through the resurrection of Jesus Christ from the dead" (1 Peter 1:3). Hence the Lord's Day is the first holyday of all and should be proposed to the devotion of the faithful and taught to them in such a way that it may become in fact a day of joy and of freedom from work. Other celebrations, unless they be truly of greatest importance, shall not have precedence over the Sunday, the foundation and core of the whole liturgical year.

— *Constitution on the Liturgy, 106*

The liturgies of morning and evening prayer are proper to every day of the week, but on Sundays we celebrate eucharist as well, a foretaste of the end of time, a chance to share in the banquet of eternity. And eucharist, as a sacrament of initiation, continually brings us back to our baptism and chrismation, reminding us that we are indeed newborns, challenging us to respond in faith to the promises we made around the holy font.

It is on the Sun's Day that we assemble, because this day is the first day, the day on which God transformed darkness into light, the day on which Christ our Savior rose from the dead. He was crucified on the eve of Saturn's Day, and on the day of the sun he appeared to his disciples and taught them all that we now offer for your examination.

— *from a sermon of Justin, second century*

One of the songs of Sunday morning prayer of the Orthodox church begins: "Now that we have witnessed the resurrection of Christ, come let us worship!" The Lord's Day is the day of resurrection, of the amazing good news that Jesus lives, of the even more amazing promise of life without end.

A Day with Many Titles

Life without end? It is here that Christians notice a paradox. The Lord's Day is the day of eternity—a span of time meant to anticipate timelessness. Time as a sign of timelessness, what a delightful contradiction! That is why Christians can call the Lord's Day "the eighth day of the week." What "eighth day" means is a day that transcends the other seven. It's as if the Lord's Day leaps out of the week altogether, as if the blessed sabbath—the seventh day—doesn't come to an end, but lasts forever.

Lord God, give us peace,
you who have given us everything!
Give us the peace of rest, the peace of the sabbath,
the peace of the day that knows no evening!

Although the world is beautiful,
although the world is so *very good,*
behold, it will wear out, it will pass away.
The world itself has a morning, and it has an evening.

But the sabbath has neither evening nor end,
for it is as holy as you are.
May we rest in you in the sabbath of eternal life!
  — *Augustine, fourth century*

That's the sense Christians bring when they call Sunday the "sabbath." That's the sense that caused Justin to announce: "The new law demands that you Christians observe a perpetual sabbath." In mystery, God has lifted all creation into endless rest, into perpetual light, where no time is ordinary, where every day is a sabbath, where every day is a feast.

That is why Christians have traditionally called the least important days on their calendar *feriae*—fair days or feast days. In the fourth century, Sylvester, a bishop of Rome, preached at length about this wonderful paradox of time. In Christ, all time is a feast. All days are sabbath. A grand coincidence (or is it?) puts Sylvester's own feast day on December 31, New Year's Eve, a day given to considering time in all its mystery. A century before Sylvester, Origen preached: "Tell me something, you people who gather at church only on feasts. Aren't all the days of the year feast days? Isn't every day the Lord's Day?"

Keeping Sunday as a day of beginnings, as a day of resurrection, as a day of the Spirit—as the Lord's Day—comes down to a rather basic challenge: We have to keep the whole day, not just an hour or so of parish liturgy. How? The possibilities are endless.

Even families that are torn up by their own busyness will often set aside certain meals, especially on Sundays, to eat together. Guests are an important part of sabbath or Lord's Day meals, and they are also valuable companions—meaning literally "those with whom we break bread"—at our more humble Friday fasting meals, as well.

One of the customs of the sabbath is to try to make sure that no one eats meals alone. A Christian saying reminds us that a guest in the home is Christ in the home.

A simple and customary way to make the Lord's Day special is to set aside "Sunday best" in clothes, in foods, in flowers, in candles and in dinnerware—especially in outgoing hospitality that seeks to gather family, friends, strangers and even the all-too-familiar on a day of peace, recreation, contentment and joy.

Keeping the Lord's Day requires the imagination of the Spirit, the creative energy of the Creator, the discipline of disciplines. It is a day to gather family and friends, to set out in new directions and to make new discoveries, to heal wounds and begin the labor required of us to restore the earth to its original goodness.

Saturday

The seventh day of the week is the sabbath day. There are two different accounts of the ten commandments—Exodus 20 and Deuteronomy 5— and in these two accounts the commandment to keep the sabbath (the seventh day, our Saturday) is worded differently:

> Remember to keep holy the sabbath day. Six days you may labor and do all your work, but the seventh is the sabbath of the Lord, your God. No work may be done then either by you, or your son or daughter, or your male or female slave, or your beast, or by the alien who lives with you. In six days the Lord made the heavens and the earth, the sea and all that is in them; but on the seventh day God rested. That is why the Lord blessed the sabbath day and made it holy.
>
> — *Exodus 20:8–11*
>
> Take care to keep holy the sabbath day as the Lord, your God, commanded you. . . . For remember that you too were once slaves in Egypt, and the Lord, your God, brought you from there with a strong hand and outstretched arm. That is why the Lord, your God, has commanded you to observe the sabbath day.
>
> — *Deuteronomy 5:12–15*

We are given two reasons to keep the sabbath day: God rested from the work of creation and God led us from slavery to freedom. Keeping the sabbath involves these two acts of praise: to God who completes creation and pronounces it very good, to God who enters into history to lead us to the land of rest.

The Lord Jesus kept the sabbath. According to the gospels (see Matthew 12:1–12; Luke 6:1–11, 13:10–17; John 5:16–18, 7:22–24), Jesus bent a few of the current rules in order to keep the spirit of the sabbath, a day of justice and compassion, a day of creation and re-creation, a day of liberation and remembrance.

Even in death, Jesus observed the sabbath. The fact of this adherence to the sabbath by the Lord Jesus in death has been lost on many Christians. The gospels use few words, but in reminding us of the sabbath rest, the gospels also remind us that the resurrection could occur only after the sabbath was past. The resurrection is the work of God, and God keeps the sabbath—resting.

Why then don't Christians keep the sabbath? Why did this holiest of days fall from our calendars? There is no answer that would be true of all Christians in all times and places. Hebrews offers an extended—if cryptic—meditation on the meaning of the sabbath for Christians (Hebrews 4). The author tells us that "a sabbath rest still remains for the people of God." Revelation 14:13 says that that kind of sabbath awaits all who die in the Lord. Just as we will share in Jesus' Friday of dying when we die and in the Lord's Day of resurrection on the final day, so, too, we are called to share in the sabbath of rest, the rest in the grave.

Very early in its history, the church developed the teaching that all time is now sabbath time, all time is rest. Christ *is* the sabbath, the day without end that completes creation. "Come to me, all you who are weary. Your souls will find rest." (Matthew 11:28–29) Christ who is the sabbath comes to remind us of the goodness of creation and the freedom to which we are called, not once a week, but every moment of every day.

> The true sabbath is not a single day, but every day. If you believe yourself to be holy simply because you keep one day of rest each week, you don't understand your duty to keep the sabbath. Only when you rest from doing evil do you keep the true sabbath, the day of delight.
> — *Justin, second century*

Gregory of Nyssa, a fourth-century bishop, reminded his people that the sabbath is the crown of creation, just as the Lord's Day is the crown of the new creation. Neither day does away with the other, "For don't you realize that the two days are sisters?"

To be true to such a tradition, Christians cannot appear to ignore the sabbath, but to make the holiness of the sabbath shine out through the week. And what better day for us to begin than the sabbath day itself? Jewish tradition tells us that on Friday evening, the sabbath descends from heaven to earth like a bride, radiant in a veil of stars.

> Come, my beloved, I sing to thy praise.
> Welcome, Bride Sabbath, the queen of our days!
> Come in thy joyousness, crown of the Lord,
> Come, bring thy peace to the folk of the world.
> — *from the song of welcome to the sabbath, "L'cha dodi"*

A Day of Rest

The sad fact is that we do ignore sabbath rest—we who probably need it most. We have created a week even the pagan Romans wouldn't recognize, without any day off, without any sort of sabbath.

Recall that we are commanded by the Most High to keep the sabbath in grateful remembrance for our liberation from slavery. But how can liberation be celebrated if we spend our "free" time in apparent subservience? A sabbath cannot happen until people learn that it's OK to spend a day doing nothing at all—like the Creator, like the Redeemer.

A day of rest can happen only through self-discipline in homes, in households, in agreements (and even in a few arguments) among employers and employees, among family and community members. Those who would wear the crown of the sabbath are those who recognize the dignity to which they are called. Those who would receive this gift from God are those who spend their lives working for the reign of God at work and at rest.

> To set apart one day a week for freedom, a day on which we would not use the instruments which have been so easily turned into weapons of destruction, a day for being with ourselves, a day of detachment from the vulgar, of independence from external obligations, a day on which we stop worshiping the idols of technical civilization, a day on which we use no money, a day of armistice in the economic struggle with our fellow humans and with the forces of nature—is there any institution that holds out greater hope for our progress than the sabbath?
> — *Abraham Heschel,* The Sabbath, Its Meaning for Modern Man

Friday

The sixth day of the week is the day God finished creation. Jesus died on the sixth day. In John's gospel we discover that Jesus also completed the work of creation. Jesus was "aware that everything was now finished" (John 19:28). So that we don't miss the comparison with the first chapters of Genesis, the author of the gospel reminds us that it is the day before the sabbath. The author then tells us of a soldier opening Jesus' side, "and immediately blood and water flowed out." Are we to remember someone else whose side was opened? The author of the gospel is speaking of the creation of Eve!

While Adam is asleep, God opens his side to create Eve as "flesh of his flesh." The blood and water flowing from Jesus' side is the new Eve, the church. Paul says that Jesus is the new Adam and that the church is indeed Jesus' bride (1 Corinthians 15:45–49, Ephesians 5:21–32). This image of bride and groom is not meant to suggest the stereotyped and chauvinistic subservience of woman to man. In fact, these images can only make sense if we believe woman and man to be equal partners, bound not by rigid obligation or oppressive social roles, but by freedom and love.

The Friday Fast

If Friday is the day we *welcome* the bride and groom, it is also the day we fast to bid *farewell* to the groom, taken from our midst on this day, sacrificed for us: "When the bridegroom is taken away from them, then they will fast in those days" (Luke 5:35). Fasting is a form of self-mortification—a word rooted in *mors*, death. In fasting together on Fridays, we are saying that we are willing to lay down our lives for each other, even as Lord Jesus laid down his life for us.

One reason for the custom of not eating meat on Fridays is as an act of respect for creation. After all, on this day all the "cattle and creeping things, and wild animals of all kinds" were created—and we, too, were created. Created on the same day, are we to devour one another? (Fish, of course, were not created on the sixth day. Devouring them on Fridays even became for Christians a way to anticipate the heavenly banquet when that largest of sea creatures, Leviathan [see Isaiah 27:1 and Psalm 74:14], the very embodiment of evil, will be slain and served up to the saved.)

Surely another reason for the Friday fast is a way to recollect the dreadful consequences of irresponsible eating in Eden. Fasting on Fridays is a sign of great sorrow for sin, the sin for which we were kicked out of Eden, the sin that took the bridegroom from us, the sin of infidelity and broken promises, whenever we turn our backs on our own baptism. What are our baptismal vows if not wedding vows? We pledge to love each other as we love Christ, as bride and groom "till death do us part."

Fasting on Friday is also a sign of great joy for grace. For we are invited to return to paradise and stand before the tree of life, the cross of Christ. In the gracious life of Easter we believe that even death will not dissolve this marriage between Christ and ourselves. It was on a Friday that the Spirit of life was breathed into dead clay (Genesis 2:7). And it was on a Friday that the Spirit of Jesus was given to us from the cross (John 19:30).

How splendid the cross of Christ!
It brings life, not death.
It brings paradise, not exile.
A tree destroyed us.
A tree now brings us life.
— *Theodore of Studios, ninth century*

Some people think that the church did away with Friday fasting, but that's simply not so. Modern church law (canons 1249–1253) challenges us to keep Fridays with fasting and abstinence from meat as well as special prayer, self-denial and works of mercy. The law permits the national conferences of bishops to be more specific about the nature of Friday observance. The bishops of the United States have done just that, asking us to pray, fast and do works of charity on Fridays for the sake of peace in our homes and communities, in our country and our world.

In the long tradition of the church, we are called to make Friday a day we dedicate to restoring the earth to Eden: in peace, in simplicity, in harmony. We are called to stop wasting both human and natural resources. We are called to wholeness, to turn away from consumerism, to stop whatever pollutes both ourselves and our planet. That perhaps is one of the most powerful reasons to fast.

Such fasting is in every sense a turning away from sin and a living of the gospel. The Friday fast is but the necessary first course to both the sabbath rest and the Sunday feast.

A Leap into Eternity

Sabbath after sabbath, through Friday fasts and Sunday feasts, Christians are formed in the mystery of the death, rest and resurrection of the Lord. This paschal mystery is the mystery of the week, of the passage of time from sabbath into eternal sabbath, from first day into eighth day. God has offered the week as a gift, first formed in the creation of the world. The gift is to count seven days and then to find that the beginning is the end.

When time has made weeks into a gentle routine, a way of life, gradually they will be perceived not as a circle, recurring round after round. Gradually they will be known for what they are—a spiral staircase, Jacob's ladder ascending into heaven.

■ *Peter Mazar*

■ CHRISTIAN YEAR

We all live our lives in cycles. There is the cycle of our own birth, maturation, aging and death. There are the similar cycles of family and close friends that, even though they are not identical to our own chronologically, still affect us deeply. There is a cycle of world events that seems to carry us along in its tide. There is the yearly cycle of work, school and civic events. There is a monthly cycle especially important to women. There is the weekly cycle of work and relaxation . . . and a daily cycle. There is the cycle of nature, which profoundly affects all the other cycles. Finally, there are the religious cycles of the day, week and year that shape our religious beliefs and practice. At one time or another, given special circumstances, one or another cycle will surface as more important. For example, many families have experienced the death of a dear one around Thanksgiving or Christmas. For them, at least for that year, the celebration of the holiday will be transposed into a different key. The same would normally happen when the birth of a child occurs, let's say, in the days surrounding Easter. Easter will be different that year.

The point of all this is that one cannot isolate one cycle from another in pure abstraction. When we try to understand something like the Christian year, we are not talking about a calendar set in stone but about the manner in which the many ways of counting time interact with one another. In fact, what we call the Christian year is the result of a long process of development that takes a great number of factors into account. In the earliest days of Christianity there was no such thing as a Christian year. There *was* a Christian week, for the disciples of Jesus and their descendants seem to have celebrated the mystery of Christ's death and resurrection by assembling for the eucharist on what we now call the Lord's Day or Sunday. But any culture will eventually shape a yearly cycle of anniversaries and commemorations precisely because it is a culture, something commonly held by a large number of people. Such annual calendars function to solidify the group's identity and purpose. A good example is the cycle of civic holidays we celebrate in the United States, holidays that emphasize an aspect of the national heritage: a significant figure, independence or the need to express gratitude for the blessing bestowed on the country. You can see already that a specific culture's celebration of its identity is going to be determined to a great extent by how it fits into society at large. Sometimes, in the larger sense, it will be countercultural; sometimes it will form the backbone of the culture at large as, for example, important days in Islam still do in traditional Islamic countries.

So when we speak of a Christian year, we are dealing with something far more complex than the fact that "Christ's saving work" is celebrated in sacred memory by the church "on appointed days in the course of year" (General Norms for the Liturgical Year and Calendar, 1). That much is true, of course, but it is far from the whole picture of what is happening when Christians really observe the calendar. I want to trace the roots of a celebration of the annual cycle to show what I mean.

Jewish Roots

Earliest Christianity arose in the midst of the rich religious culture of Judaism, one that naturally had its own cycle of feasts. By our Lord's time the people of Israel celebrated three major pilgrimage feasts: Passover, Weeks and Tabernacles.

Passover. Passover took place in the month of Nisan, the first full moon of spring. Its origins were both nomadic and agricultural: nomadic in that it marked the sacrifice of a young male sheep and agricultural in that the first sheaf of the barley harvest was sacrificed. Both events took place in the early spring, and so the feasts of *Pesach* (the sacrifice of the lamb) and of *Mazzoth* (unleavened bread) were combined. By Jesus' time this feast had acquired an important religious significance. It celebrated the delivery of Israel from Egyptian bondage in the Exodus.

The gospels make a good deal of the fact that Jesus was crucified at this time. In the synoptics Jesus celebrates the Passover meal with his disciples on the night of his betrayal, thus leaving them with a ritual way to remember the significance of his passion, death and resurrection. In John, on the other hand, Jesus himself represents the paschal lamb, for he dies at the same time that the lambs are slaughtered. We shall come back to this difference in the timing of these final events in our Lord's life later. That Passover is important because the Christian understanding of Jesus is underlined by Paul's use of this image even in writing to a non-Jewish congregation:

> For Christ, our paschal lamb, has been sacrificed. Let us therefore celebrate the festival, not with the old leaven, the leaven of malice and evil, but with the unleavened bread of sincerity and truth.
> — 1 Corinthians 5:7–8

Weeks. The second great pilgrimage festival was that of Weeks. The Hebrew name for the feast was *Shavuoth*, which means seven weeks plus one day, because it took place 50 days after Passover. The word Pentecost comes from the Greek translation of the Hebrew Shavuoth. The first day of the feast was always on the first day of the week, Sunday, rather than on on the seventh day of the week, Shabbat (Sabbath) or Saturday. Weeks was agricultural in origin, a feast of thanksgiving for the harvest. By Jesus' time its meaning had changed to commemorate the giving of the law at Sinai.

Tabernacles. The third pilgrimage feast was called Tabernacles. This, too, had its origins as an agricultural feast celebrating the harvest of grapes. It was called variously *Asiph* (Ingathering) or, because during harvesttime Israelites lived in huts out in the fields, it was also called *Sukkoth* (Tabernacles). Once again, by the time of Jesus, what was originally an agricultural feast was theologized to celebrate the enthronement of the Lord God of Israel and therefore was associated closely with the Temple.

Each of these feasts strongly influenced the development of the Christian year. But it is important to remember that as feasts of pilgrimage they were focused on a specific geographic place: Jerusalem and its Temple. Together with the weekly celebration of the Sabbath and several other annual celebrations, these feasts contributed greatly to build the cultural world in which the faith of the earliest Christians matured. Of course, the roots of Christianity were not limited to Israelite culture, as Paul's epistles show. Eventually Christians dealt with many cultures as the gospel spread. This cultural dialogue involved Christians from the very beginning, and Christians still dialogue with cultures today. At no time did Christian belief or practice develop in a cultural vacuum.

The Development of the Liturgical Year

We mentioned previously that a liturgical year did not exist in earliest Christianity. As a matter of fact it seems that for some time Christians had no annual feasts at all. There were probably several reasons for this. First, newly founded groups tend not to need a great deal of structure either in their governance or in the way they celebrate time. Second, Christmas belonged to a movement that for the most part had to remain clandestine as far as public expressions were concerned. Third, the weekly Sunday assembly provided an adequate source of identity for the group.

Pascha. Toward the end of the second century we become aware of an annual feast of Easter, *Pascha,* celebrated throughout the church. There was strong disagreement among the churches as to when this celebration should take place. It seems that even early in the century the churches of Asia Minor had begun to celebrate Pascha on whatever day of the week the Jewish Passover fell. Because the Jews reckoned by a lunar calendar and not by the dates of the solar calendar with which we are familiar, it became necessary to assign a solar calendar date to the celebration. The church at

Rome had considerable difficulty over this practice, insisting that the Paschal Vigil be celebrated so as to conclude on a Sunday, the day of the Lord's resurrection. It may well be, however, that the annual Sunday celebration at Rome was a relatively recent innovation. The Roman church may not have celebrated any annual feasts prior to the middle of the second century.

It is important to note that the earliest celebration of Pascha was what we have come to call a unitive feast. It did not parcel out the events of Jesus' passion, death and resurrection on several days but rather celebrated the whole event of Jesus Christ from incarnation to ascension in one feast that also looked forward to his final coming. That the Christians of Asia Minor celebrated the feast on the actual (lunar) anniversary of Christ's death meant, however, that they would concentrate in particular on the passion and death of the Lord, while the Western celebration on Saturday night-Sunday tended to focus more explicitly on the resurrection.

Within a short time of this late second-century debate we know of the practice of celebrating the 50 days after Easter as a festal period. As yet Pentecost was not a distinct feast but marked the end of the joyful season. Fasting and kneeling, two signs of penance, were not allowed during the fifty days.

Lent. In the third century we have the first witnesses to the celebration of baptism at the Paschal Vigil. This sensible alliance of Pascha and initiation probably encouraged the extension of the prepaschal fast first to a week, then to three weeks (as in the case of Rome) and finally to the 40-day Lent with which we are familiar.

Recent scholarship has suggested, however, that the Egyptian church may originally have celebrated initiation on a different day. The Egyptian 40-day Lent may not at first have been tied to Pascha at all but rather followed immediately upon the celebration of Epiphany (in Egypt, the celebration of the Lord's baptism) in imitation of Jesus' fast for 40 days in the desert following his baptism (Matthew 3:17—4:2, Mark 1:11–13, Luke 3:22; 4:1–2). Lent itself has had a fascinating history, heavily dependent on a local custom (especially in the church of Rome) and in the waning fortunes of adult initiation at Easter with the subsequent emphasis placed on the recovery of baptismal innocence and zeal by means of penitential practice.

A major turning point in the development of the liturgical year was inspired by the acceptance of the Christian faith by the Roman emperor

Constantine in 312 CE. The fourth century was to see the first full-bloom Christian year. The reasons for this are not hard to find. We remarked earlier that public celebration of feasts was somewhat curtailed by the clandestine nature of an illegal sect. Now, however, the tables had turned, and Christians became not only publicly acceptable but also publicly triumphant in a number of cities around the Mediterranean. With the public areas of a number of cities (Rome with its encrusted pagan aristocracy was to remain somewhat of an exception) now at their disposal, Christians were much freer to create the kind of festal calendar suitable to a religion that had now taken on civic significance.

This is not to argue, as has been popular for some time, that there was a drastic revolution in the Christian sense of time in the fourth century. Recently several scholars have seriously questioned Gregory Dix's theory that with Constantine came a new Christian attitude toward time—one that was no longer keenly interested in time coming to an end in Christ (eschatology, a focus on the ultimate future) but rather in settling in to the world as it is (historicization, a focus on the present time). The problem with Dix's theory is that it ignores the fact that the earliest feasts about which we know (and perhaps even the early Egyptian Lent) were explicitly geared to historical commemoration as well as eschatological hope.

Christmas and Epiphany. There were several developments in the Christian year during the fourth century that are worth mentioning. First, Christians began to celebrate a special feast commemorating the incarnation of Christ. In the West Christmas was celebrated on December 25, the former date of the pagan feast of the birth of the unconquered Sun (*sol invictus*). We know of its existence from at least 336 CE. It is difficult to say whether the pagan feast inspired Christians to create a counterfeast, the birth of the *real* light of the world, or whether the dating of Christmas relied on an elaborate calculation that marked the passion of Christ (by some, traditionally dated March 25) with this conception, thus making his life a perfect whole. Whatever the exact historical inspiration, it is clear that the old pagan feast provided a most convenient day to celebrate the birth of Christ. Interestingly, Christmas, too, was a unitive feast at this time, celebrating the incarnation as a whole. We know that, because in Rome the original gospel reading for Christmas Day was the prologue to the Gospel of John (John 1:1–18), as it is today in the Roman rite (Christmas, Mass during the Day).

The earliest Eastern celebration of the incarnation took place on January 6 and was called Epiphany (manifestation). Some scholars date this celebration as early as the third century, but there is direct evidence of the feast from sources dated only to the fourth century and later. Different local churches celebrated Epiphany with different focuses: the nativity of the Lord (Jerusalem) or his baptism (Egypt). The church at Jerusalem celebrated the feast for eight days (an octave), beginning at Bethlehem and using different churches each day for eucharistic celebrations.

By the late fourth century East and West had exchanged feasts. Easterners (with the exception of Jerusalem for a time and Armenia permanently) accepted December 25 for the Nativity, and westerners adopted January 6 for Epiphany. In the West, however, the feast was not focused on the baptism of Jesus but rather on the visit of the magi (Rome) and the "three miracles" (magi in France, baptism in Spain and the miracle of Cana in northern Italy).

The Easter Triduum. The second major development of the Christian year in the course of the fourth century was the expansion of the Paschal Vigil to what we now know as the Easter Triduum. The church at Jerusalem seems to have been the innovator, probably because Jerusalem was the place where the events of Jesus' passion, death and resurrection occurred. A fourth-century pilgrim, the Spanish religious woman Egeria wrote a detailed account of the entire liturgical year, particularly of the Triduum, in her diary (381–84 CE). Palm Sunday at Jerusalem involved such celebrations as a long procession down the Mount of Olives to the city in the afternoon. On Tuesday evening the faithful held a vigil at the Mount of Olives commemorating the Lord's discourse to his apostles (Matthew 24:1—26:2). There was a double celebration of the eucharist on the afternoon of Holy Thursday in the large church that Constantine built at Golgotha. During the night between Holy Thursday and Good Friday there was another vigil with a procession down the Mount of Olives to Gethsemane and from there to Golgotha and the complex of shrines at the Holy Sepulchre. There was veneration of the cross in the small chapel at Golgotha the morning of Good Friday, with three hours of readings, psalms and all four passion accounts between noon and 3:00 PM. Finally, there was the great Easter Vigil itself at which the elect were baptized and invited to the eucharist for their first time. The Vigil ended early in the morning on Easter Sunday.

Needless to say, the many liturgies surrounding the Triduum in Jerusalem provided an exhaustive itinerary culminating in the drama of salvation history. Perhaps only the most enthusiastic and pious could keep up with everything.

Advent. There is one other season that needs to be discussed here: the time of preparation for Christmas that we call Advent. The Christian East has never known a formal liturgical season of Advent comparable to ours in the West. The West most likely developed a season of preparation originally geared toward initiation at Epiphany, hence a 40-day fast beginning on St. Martin's Day, November 11. From a season of six weeks in length, it gradually shortened to four. Before the current liturgical color scheme was adopted, a twelfth-century witness called for the use of a somber penitential color in Advent. The Missal of Pius V (1570) settled on violet, which remains the official color in the Roman rite today. In the Roman rite, however, Advent has always been understood, with some local exceptions, more as a season of preparation than of penitence.

The story of the medieval development of the Christian year is basically the elaboration of the major feasts and seasons we have discussed here. The calendar gradually filled up with saints' days and devotional feasts—the Precious Blood of Christ, Christ the King, Trinity Sunday, Holy Family, Corpus Christi, Sacred Heart or the Seven Sorrows of the Blessed Virgin Mary—that were devoted not to an event within salvation history but to certain ideas that captured Christian imagination. In the medieval period there was also a tendency to replace Sunday, the Lord's Day as such (the days for celebrating the paschal mystery), with special commemorations.

Calendars are like gardens. Eventually they get cluttered and need pruning. Every now and then pruning (reform) takes place. We are living in one such period.

The Christian Year Today

There are several significant dimensions of the reform of the Christian year that was inspired by the Second Vatican Council and codified in the document, General Norms for the Liturgical Year and Calendar (1969). Sunday has been restored to its preeminence as the original feast, the Lord's Day. Great emphasis has been put on the Easter Triduum as the high point of the liturgical year. Lent has a double focus in the preparation of the elect for initiation at the Paschal Vigil and a period of common penance for everyone else in the church as we prepare to join in solidarity with the neophytes by reaffirming our baptismal commitment. An effort has been made to revive the great Fifty Days of Eastertime as a period of immense joy for the church. Its risen Savior is present within each member. In this mystagogical period, young and old reflect with wonderment on the meaning of their ritual initiation and of their experience of Christian life. Now we see Advent clearly as a period of preparation to celebrate the incarnation of the Lord. It is not really penitential. The Christmas season is unified by the concluding feast of the Baptism of the Lord on the Sunday after Epiphany.

Last, and very important, local churches are encouraged to develop their own particular calendars within the context of the church's general calendar. In other words, we are asked to set aside several days that are characteristic of our own historical community's incorporation into Christian faith as a whole. This is usually accomplished by celebrating feasts of saints or moments in the life of the Lord that have special meaning for our community. This may take the form of a special observance of the patron of a parish church or of a religious order. More and more, communities are stretching the boundaries of the calendar to include their own celebrations on important days like the national memorial day of Dr. Martin Luther King, Jr., or like a day of prayer for peace on the feast of the Transfiguration, which by poignant irony falls on August 6, the anniversary of the dropping of the first atomic bomb on Hiroshima.

We began by considering the inescapable fact that a number of cycles give shape to our lives, some of them private and some public. By now it should be clear that the Christian year has a cycle that is peculiarly its own and challenges us to decisions.

For example, will a family go to visit parents or in-laws at some distance or stay home to celebrate the Paschal Vigil and sacraments of initiation in their own parish when they have become committed to the catechumenate and very much attached to the candidates for initiation? When the obligations of work or civic responsibilities conflict with special celebrations of my local community, what kind of choice will I make?

There are no simple answers to these questions, nor is there a once-and-for-all, valid-for-all-time articulation of the Christian year, for the liturgical year partakes of that curious tension that characterizes all of our

Christian life. It is a way of being inserted into a reality that is much larger than ourselves, into a community that forms us. At the same time, it is shaped by the people who celebrate it in their own social, economic and political circumstances. It is, to say it briefly, both our heritage as faith-filled Christians and very much what we make of it.

▪ *John F. Baldovin*

■ INITIATION IN THE CHURCH YEAR

The questions we need to ask about initiation and the calendar are those raised in the gospel, in Jesus' parable about the rich man who decided to build extra barns and was told, "You fool! This night your life is required of you!" It is raised by Jesus' question about what it profits to gain the whole world but suffer the loss of one's soul. It is raised by his words about the lilies of the field and the birds of the sky which neither sow nor reap. Clearly, Jesus had his own sense of time, different from that with which we usually operate.

Time

There are many ways of looking at time. On the one hand, there is measured time, our time, the time we have to fill, the time we have to do things and to get things done. But then there is another dimension of time in which we live but that we cannot schedule and that we cannot control: the time it takes for wounds to heal, for wisdom to be learned, for grief to be assuaged, for love to blossom, for conversion to occur. These are things that happen without our planning, things that affect us most profoundly but are out of our control. These are things that occur "in due time" or, better, "in God's good time." So there is our time, the time we call our own; and there is God's time. And we live in both. They are not separate times but two dimensions of our own life in time. The one, admittedly, occupies the surface of our lives, the other, God's time, seems like the deep undercurrent of our days, so deep we often forget it until it erupts into our own time, and our schedules are disrupted, our calendars thrown into chaos.

St. Augustine wrote in his *Confessions* concerning time: "If you do not ask me, I know what it is; if you ask me, I do not know." We are all familiar with time, but what it is none of us can say with precision. Yet there is a conviction about it that is important to our tradition. God made the earth and all that is in it and placed our first parents on it and said, indicating the spaciousness of the earth: "Be fruitful and increase, fill the earth and subdue it." In other words, God gave us space and place for our own. But God never gave us time. Time remains God's property, lent to us grudgingly. We can never really save time or accumulate it or spend it as if we had a wealth of it. The past is already taken from us; the future is not yet given to us; we have only now. And even that does not belong to us. It belongs to God.

Religious conversion, therefore, would seem to involve a conversion in the way we think about time. In the precatechumenate, surely, the questions the church needs to ask of the inquirer are: What time is it for you? What time is it in your life? And in the catechumenate itself, coming to terms with how we relate to time: How do you use it? For what do you think it is given to you? These are questions that get to the heart of our relationship with the world, with ourselves, with God. Can there be any genuine conversion that does not come to grips with the issue of time, to a vivid understanding of "God's good time"? Isn't an acceptance of God's time another way of saying, "Thy will be done"? Can a person come to know God without discovering what time really is in human life?

Calendar

Then there is the calendar. The very idea of a calendar is fascinating: time divided up into blank spaces to be filled in, time represented as space, giving us the illusion that we have blocks of time, as we have blocks of space, to occupy as we will. As we fill it in, we create a mirror image of our lives. Look at our calendar, our date book, our schedule, and we will see *ourselves*. Like a fingerprint, it can identify us.

There are others, of course, who help fill in our calendars for us. We buy a calendar and it is already marked up: Washington's birthday, end of the financial quarter, opening of the grouse season. Calendars are essentially social institutions, recording things that people do together, observances held in common. Consequently, every group has its own calendar, marking the times important to its members. A calendar represents not just our "strictly personal commitments" but our involvement in the communities to which we belong. The calendar of each community reveals its identity: financial calendars, business calendars, sports calendars, school calendars, religious calendars. Each reveals purposes, goals, values, corporate symbols.

There was a time in European history when the church's calendar, the liturgical year, was everyone's calendar and effectively served to organize the life of society as a whole. The very word "holiday," from holy day, reminds us of it. But now we live in the confusion of conflicting calendars. Is it Candlemas Day or Groundhog Day on February 2? Yet the value of the church's calendar should not be overlooked. We tend to dismiss Easter and Christmas Catholics, but they are people who still feel some sense of identity with the Christian community. Sometimes, at least, they know what day it is and the Christian calendar pulls them back. To be a Catholic is to live by the Catholic calendar, and the depth of our Catholic identity cannot be divorced from the role the church's calendar plays in our lives.

To become a Catholic, then, one of the first things a person needs to do is to be introduced to our calendar. Children love to be told that there are feasts to anticipate and to be introduced to celebrations that recur. (They have a wonderful sense of rhythm and ritual.) Should this not also happen in the catechumenate? If the calendar is a primary expression of our communal identity, shouldn't we give newly admitted catechumens a blank calendar and sit down with them individually and help them fill in the seasons of the year, the days of festivity and fast, the holy days, the saints days and the special observances?

The clash of calendars provides an opportunity for us to examine the seriousness of our commitment. A couple of years ago in our parish, the Friday night fasting supper, observed by parishioners during Lent, had to be moved from the parish hall to the church basement because the parish school had scheduled a dance for the eighth graders. In another parish, the seventh Sunday of Easter fell on Memorial Day weekend and the VFWs greeted the arriving parishioners with an honor guard of fixed bayonets. It was also "Communications Sunday," so the sermon was preempted by a tape recording of the appeal by Archbishop Fulton Sheen. It was communion Sunday for the Brownies, who took part in the entrance procession, walking in pairs and holding hands, with the fixed bayonets right behind them! Such clashes of calendars are not just purely logistical problems but represent a clash of values.

Something Has To Give

There is a profound paradox in the church's calendar. St. Jerome recognized the paradox centuries ago when he remarked that all time belongs to the Lord and therefore there really are no holy days, no day is holier than any other in Christianity. Grace knows no season, for this is the new age when the Spirit is poured out without restriction. Jerome writes:

> If you want to go into the matter more deeply, then you still have to say that all days are equal, that Christ is not crucified on Good Friday alone, that he did not rise just on Easter Sunday, but that every day is the day of his resurrection and a day for eating his flesh. Sundays and fast days had to be instituted by prudent persons for the sake of those who live more for this world than for God and cannot—indeed, will not—spend all their time in church, offering to God the sacrifice of their prayers before engaging in any human undertaking. So, it would be quite in order for us to fast always and to pray without ceasing, rejoicing with those who rejoice on the Lord's day, having received the Body of the Lord.

Here is the distinction between "our time" and "God's good time"! All time is God's good time, and ideally that would be the only time we would live by. That is what makes the church calendar different from any other. While it sets apart days and schedules liturgical assemblies, it does so that we might call to consciousness the fact that all time belongs to God and is the channel of God's redemptive purposes. So the Christian calendar commemorates times past—the historic events of our salvation, the wondrous transformation of the lives of men and women—not for their own sake but as a promise for the future. In remembering the past and allowing it to shape our hopes for the future, the Christian calendar calls us day by day to remember that now, this day, our time is really the time of God. Now is the now of God where past and future meet and become one. "Oh, if today you hear God's voice," says the opening psalm of the Christian day, "harden not your hearts." Whereas other calendars are intended to help us find ways to divide our own time, the Christian calendar exists only to transform time into God's time.

Eternity

For centuries the church's baptismal liturgy, and now the Rite of Acceptance to the Order of Catechumens, has begun with the question: "What do you ask of the church of God?"

"Faith."

"And what does faith give you?"

"Eternal life."

There are certain experiences in the lives of individuals and communities that we have come to call "peak experiences." These are moments of ecstasy, in which life seems so full that nothing more is desired, nothing more is needed. One thinks of instances such as the achievement of success, or moments of loving and of being loved, or of a nation's victory in war, or the gift of freedom to the imprisoned or to oppressed peoples. At such time nothing more could be asked for. Such moments, I suggest, are glimpses of eternal life.

Eternal life is not so much the cessation of time—when time stops—as it is the utter fullness of time. Time is so complete that no future is needed, for there is nothing to be added. Time is so complete that the past—so riddled with mistakes, with lost opportunities, with sin—is now made good and given back—"ransomed, healed, restored, forgiven." These are times so perfect that we say, "I could have died and gone to heaven." Such moments, I believe, are intimations of eternity, of the life for which we are destined. And this life is for us *now*.

In his most solemn fashion, Jesus tells us: "Truly, truly, I say to you: whoever believes *has* eternal life" (John 6:47). And here is the heart of the matter. Baptism and eucharist are community events. They have to be scheduled. They have to be written on the calendar. Yet they promise the gift of the fullness of time, the gift of eternal life. Such a gift, of its nature, occurs in God's good time, not in ours. We can schedule the rite, but we cannot schedule the gift. The rite and calendar prepare us for the gift by putting us in a position where we can receive it.

In Rosemary Haughton's terms: The calendar of the church and its rituals are the means of our formation, but it is a formation that must be open to transformation. The calendar of the church year is a discipline, an apprenticeship, an ongoing exercise that raises our consciousness of that dimension of life we have called "God's good time." To the degree that we are shaped by it, live our lives in harmony with its themes, we are open to the transformation that happens in God's good time.

The Easter Triduum

It is a common and understandable but ultimately misleading practice to begin discussing the liturgical year by speaking about Advent. It is understandable because that's where our liturgical books start. But the real beginning of the liturgical year is Easter, the Paschal Triduum—it begins where it ends: with death and resurrection.

Eternal life is when things happen in God's good time, when God— in whom past, present and future are not merely *as* one but *are* one— breaks into our time. Here at the Easter ambo, font and altar we experience eternity erupting in our midst. These holy and archaic rituals bring into our time the dawn of creation, the Exodus, the Jordan, the sacramental practices of centuries. And they gather in the future: the pure, bright waters running through the streets of the new Jerusalem, and the table in the kingdom of God where we shall take our places with Abraham, Isaac and Jacob. In so doing, they also gather up the whole lifetime of the candidates for baptism, restoring to them fresh the years of wandering and sin and blindness. Death, their final destiny, is already put behind them as they rise with Christ to eternity. Easter is the beginning and the end, the center and summation of the whole Christian year, of the whole Christian life. From this point, historically and theologically, the rest of the calendar ripples out.

Backwards into Lent

Lent has no other goal than the Easter sacraments. If past and future meet at the Paschal Triduum, Lent is for recovering the past and Eastertime for living the future. In Lent, we pick up the pieces of lives undone by sin. Those elected for baptism are set, with the whole community, under the sign of the temptations in the desert. Like Jesus Christ, the beloved of God are driven into the wilderness by the Spirit.

Lent is a wilderness of our own making. According to exegetes, the wilderness experience of Jesus was a reliving of the dependency of Israel on its God. For us it is a reliving of our own dependency. Under the images of the great lenten gospels we acknowledge as our own the thirst of the woman at the well, the blindness of the man Jesus alone could heal, the dying and corruption of Lazarus. Lent invites the elect and the faithful to look at their lives, their life histories, and know their need for the grace of him who alone could quench thirst, open eyes, deliver from death.

And Forward Through Eastertime

Eastertime is grace abounding: 50 days of rejoicing to overwhelm 40 days of repentance. Its character flows from time so full that no more could be sought. The past has been raised, anointed, decked in splendor, and we are invited to take our places at the wedding feast of the Lamb. Already we live the life of the world to come. We need no more. The fathers of the church used to speak of this season of 50 days as but a single day, the eighth day, symbol of eternal life. Eastertime is a season for the newly baptized to assimilate Easter mysteries in sharing the word, the eucharist and the fellowship of all the baptized. It is also a time for them to learn to live in this world as people who have put death behind them.

Advent and Christmastime

According to *our* calendar, Christmas begins in the evening of December 24 and lasts until the Sunday after Epiphany, when we celebrate the baptism of the Lord. In the world, Christmas begins after Thanksgiving and ends on December 25. There is not only a clash of calendars but a clash of cultures—a clash so violent that one wonders whether the Christian feast of Christmas, with its time of preparation and then celebration, can possibly survive.

Have we given up? Are we resigned to singing carols and attending parties until Christmas Day and then throwing out the tree? Are we aware of the Christian significance of the tree, the wreath, the open-door hospitality and festive foods? Are we capable of initiating others into the Christian meaning of symbols? Time itself is our major sacrament, and to yield on these matters may be equivalent to giving up on our calendar altogether.

What a profound loss that would be! What Advent and Christmas celebrate is the redemption of time itself. Advent calls us to ponder the meaning of the history of our race and the possibility of that history being redeemed. In its paradoxical way, it confronts us with past and future at the same time: the ancient longings of Israel and the eschatological longings of the human race.

Christmas in the Christian calendar confronts us with the problem of time itself. It is not to be confused with the secular feast and its glut of *Gemütlichkeit,* for it confronts us with the profound paradox of one who came, is coming and will come again—the paradox of triumph through weakness, salvation through a child. One would do well to sing our traditional carols, especially those medieval songs that speak not of "chestnuts roasting on an open fire" but of sin and redemption, birth and death, poverty and majesty, echoing the scriptures themselves.

Discipline of the Calendar

Catholic Christianity is not a direct and immediate relationship with God but a relationship mediated through the symbols, forms, practices and ethos of our Catholic culture and tradition. It cannot be stressed too much that Christianity is incarnational. Christianity claims that God entered our world and our history in the flesh of Jesus of Nazareth. God is to be found, heard and encountered in the community that is a sacrament of the continuing presence of Christ.

Consequently, anyone called to encounter God in Christ in the Catholic community will have to be initiated into the symbols, forms, practices and ethos of our community. Not only Catholic doctrine, but Catholic culture also, is needed as a medium for our assimilation to Christ. Converts need to be introduced as much, if not more, to what Catholics *do* as to what Catholics believe. All too often in religious education, we get the emphasis wrong: We may teach doctrine in a classroom and then hold dances on the Fridays of Lent. We don't take the calendar seriously. Best becomes the enemy of good when people are exhorted to sanctify without being taught the nuts and bolts of Catholic practices that are paths to sanctity. Formation means training, and training takes time and repetition. Another word for it is "discipline." Observing feasts and fasts, living the seasons of the liturgical year, is part of that discipline.

■ *Mark Searle*

Marie Adélaïde de Bethune with Grandfather Georges Terlinden.

■ THE CHRISTIAN LIFE SPAN

First, let me tell you about my coffin. No, I am not being morbid. But when I was 28 I became aware that the funeral industry was producing what they called "caskets"—real caskets are jewel boxes, small, precious—to bury the bodies of people who had died. I was so enraged by this euphemism and by the whole hypocritical approach to death, contrived by the folk art of the undertakers' fraternity and the gullible bereaved public, that I set about to make my own coffin in revolt.

The last thing I wanted was to be caught dead in a plush, lined coffin!

My carpentry skills were limited. I could not do elegant dovetails, but I could put a solid chest together. Why did the time seem right? In the attic I found an old cupboard door, 5½' x 1½', to form the base, and my mother bought secondhand shelves, wide pine boards, from a store that was closing down. It was 1942, the first year of the United States involvement in World War II.

Coffin As Incentive

Forty-five years later, my "hope chest" still graces the front hall, filled with remnants and incomplete sewing projects. Its sturdy rope handles, spliced under the instruction of an old Newport sea captain, are still in place. Its sketchy paintings have faded somewhat but still tell their story.

The sides of the coffin depict the Eternal City, shown as houses in which I have lived happily on God's lovely planet earth. On one end there is a symbol of the Gate of Heaven, cracked open a bit to let me in. On the other, a portrayal of the throne of my judge, the Good Judge who vindicated me, paid the ransom on my behalf and pointed the way for me by rising from the dead and ascending into the heavens.

On the lid the Holy Cross is surrounded with the words of the Preface of Christian Death I in Latin:

> TUIS ENIM FIDELIBUS, DOMINE,
> VITA MUTATUR, NON TOLLITUR,
> ET DISSOLUTA TERRESTRIS HUJUS INCOLATUS DOMO,
> AETERNA IN COELIS HABITATIO COMPARATUR.

The current English translation of these noble words seems, shall we say, inadequate:

> LORD, FOR YOUR FAITHFUL PEOPLE
> LIFE IS CHANGED, NOT ENDED.
> WHEN THE BODY OF OUR EARTHLY DWELLING LIES IN DEATH,
> WE GAIN AN EVERLASTING DWELLING PLACE IN HEAVEN.

Yes, I am ready to go. The inscription on both sides of the coffin is from Psalm 122 in Latin:

> I REJOICED WHEN THEY TOLD ME:
> "UP! TO THE HOUSE OF THE LORD! LET'S GO!"

At the same time I gladly remain here as long as the Lord wills. With the Lord's help I aim to put my remaining time to good use.

One problem. The coffin I made at 28 is not very wide. In fact, it is quite narrow. Over the years I have had to avoid gaining weight. After all this fuss it would be disastrous for my next of kin should Aunt Ade's lifeless frame no longer fit into the coffin she prepared so long ago by the work of her own hands. Many think it a hilarious inducement for watching one's weight. I agree. But let me add that fitting into clothes can be an equally comical incentive.

Life: Long or Short?

Is a long life desirable? In some ways I think it is. Even the Reverend Doctor Martin Luther King, Jr., on the morning before he was slain by an assassin's bullet, proclaimed with no illusion in his voice, "Longevity has its place."

A long life gives you repeated chances to learn, to observe, to experience, to listen, to obey. You do not necessarily gain new insights, but you learn the timeless ones anew, and you have an opportunity to apply them to new situations.

"Life is short," said Hippocrates, "and the art of medicine is long; experience is deceptive; opportunity is fleeting, and judgment is difficult."

Even to an elder like myself, life seems but a brief moment. "Time flies." "Where has time gone?" On this good earth, days follow days and years follow years with appointed regularity, though it seems increasingly fast.

Don't they say also that by every seventh year of life the human body has renewed all its cells? By now, then, my body must have been renewed ten times. Yet, something of its form and personality remains constant throughout the continuing flow of renewal.

That cute two-year-old girl whose thoughts I remember so well, whose body I still inhabit, sometimes seems so far away, almost another person, but one whose uniqueness is still with me.

Damasus Winzen, OSB, used to point out wisely that you never get rid of your character defects. I find myself agreeing with him more and more. Have no illusion: Your weaknesses stay with you through the years. The point is to accept them realistically, not to think you can vanquish them — they are built in — rather, learn to defuse them, to extract strength from them and try to harness this strength for good. How do I do that? As soon as I learned to accept one of my weaknesses realistically and completely, it had a way of falling into perspective for me. I would fight the weakness as smart and hard as any one, but that did not help a bit. Only acceptance set things right for me, or, as St. Paul said more convincingly than I can: "Not I, but Christ in me."

God Is Merciful

How did I learn about God's incredible mercy? It was a fine, clear day in my native Brussels. I was five, and piles of china stored in Grandfather's house throughout the years of World War I had to be moved to our smaller house next door. Mother and the two helpers were busy, and I wanted desperately to be involved in this important task.

Mother did not even hesitate. "All right, darling, here is something you may carry." She entrusted me with what looked like a precious piece of crockery. The inevitable happened. Going down the flight of stone steps in front of Grandfather's house a klutzy little girl who was trying so hard to clutch a "breakable" met with disaster. Broken pieces everywhere.

Mother was 38 then, an energetic person to whom patience did not come easily. She just went through five years of the wartime occupation, was jailed as a political prisoner and now expected her fifth child. How could I imagine that to her, all those dishes and white elephants were something of an emotional burden? But she thought of me, her child.

"That's all right, darling," she said. "You may go home now. Take care to wash the blood off your knee. Thank you for your help. And here is a reward for you." She placed into my hands a china plant holder in the shape of a swan.

Overwhelming! Here I was, fully deserving punishment, I thought, yet forgiven nevertheless. What's more, I was thanked for helping. "Helping?" I knew better than that. And to top it all off, I was even given a "reward" that I esteemed a thing of beauty, a treasure.

No one can ever preach to me about God's imagined mercy. I feel it in my bones. If a human mother can be so forgiving, can wipe away a misdeed—though the accident resulted from overeager goodwill, still my pride saw in it only failure—if she can reward a broken heart with an extra gift, how much more forgiving must be that great mother in the sky, the Lord God. "God's superabundant mercy flows on without end."

A long life also affords me the opportunity to make friends with my unique body. It allows me to come to terms with the fruit of my parents' genes, with all those strengths and handicaps, the body that God lent me to live in for a life span. If I have the use of something on loan, I must care for it with love.

To Love with No Strings Attached

In a dialogue with St. Catherine of Siena, the Lord said to her: "I have placed you in the midst of your fellows so that you might do for them what you cannot do for me, that is, love them without any hope of return."

God loves us without any hope of return! How on earth can we love God with that same essential love that expects nothing back?

Well, God's answer is simple. Pretend you are looking at your fellow human beings through God's eyes; love them as God loves them, with that same kind of pure, simple, selfless, patient, undemanding love that gives without expectation, asking nothing in return.

The longer I live, the more this truth is revealed to me in every circumstance. It rises from every page of Scripture. It is illustrated in the lives of saints. To an upside-down world, it gives straight, yet invisible bearings.

Dorothy and People

Dorothy Day, whom I met about the time of my 20th birthday around New Year's 1934, was, to me, a living example of the love that rejoices or pities but asks nothing in return. Dorothy was not without defects; her virtue was her ability to see people in a divine light that, naturally, seemed unrealistic to many.

Dorothy's family name was Day, an appropriate name for one so gifted in reporting the present moment. Basically, she was a journalist, a reporter. She wrote and she wrote. That was her craft. Did she report the discovery of great abstract theories? No. She wrote about people, plain people, unheralded people, people involved in problems, people hanging on to their dignity. What they had done was perhaps insignificant. But in their small actions, seen day by day, Dorothy perceived humanity, goodwill. She had to write about it, often flavoring compassion with keen observation and humor. Let me give you some of her typical vignettes:

> One day last summer, I saw a man sitting down by one of the piers, all alone. He sat on a log, and before him was a wooden box on which he had spread out on a paper his meager supper. He sat there and ate with some pretense at human dignity, and it was one of the saddest sights I have ever seen.
> — *The Catholic Worker*, January 1934, 3, "Commentary Column"

> This is the spirit—to recognize the significance of every small advance, and to be grateful for it. To be satisfied to work from the ground up. That is literally what Mike is doing. For the floor being of cement and the winter cold, Mike and his friends had to cover it with layer after layer of newspapers, old linoleum, boards, anything in fact that would mitigate the cold.
> The supper served us was a splendid one. For a friend of Mike's, Mrs. Thompson, who lives in the neighborhood and in her zeal reminds me of those early Christian women who helped spread Christianity, came in and made a feast of chile con carne, hot with peppers and, just what we needed to warm our innards, hot biscuits and large pots of coffee.
> — *The Catholic Worker*, March 1934, 5, "Day by Day"

> She told me about her friend who, also down and out, went to take a room or a bed in Harlem, was seduced by a young Spanish American and threw herself under a subway train a week later.
> Her lips were trembling as she talked (it was only 8:30 AM), so I invited her out to have a cup of coffee.
> — *The Catholic Worker*, June 1934, 7, "Day after Day"

> Vegetable soup—that's Peter's old standby. So yesterday, Sunday, when he came down to spend the day at the office on 15th Street, we made a huge kettle of a soup, the like of which he had never seen before: a can of beets, a chopped cucumber, green-topped onions, hard-boiled egg, potatoes and sour cream. All mixed together, a little dill chopped up on top and made good and cold in the icebox. It was a delicious feed for a hot day. We had enough for breakfast, dinner and supper.
> — *The Catholic Worker*, July–August 1934, 4, "Day after Day"

> There is none so poor that he cannot help his fellows. We have a friend down the street who lives in a little apartment for about 12 dollars a month. When she can get the work to do, she does housework, day work, the hardest kind, to earn her bread. She brought in some men's shoes and clothes that she had begged for us from her employers. Another woman in the neighborhood who has four children, a husband with a fractured skull and yet does not have the necessities of life, brought in some children's clothes to be passed on. Another mother, on relief herself, brought in some children's coats.
> — *The Catholic Worker*, October 1934, "Editorial"

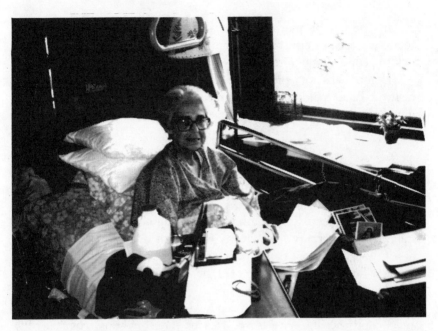

Ade Bethune: artist, theologian, consultant, Christian

We had a mad friend once, a Jewish worker from the East Side, who wore a rosary around his neck and came to us reciting the Psalms in Hebrew. He stayed with us for weeks at a time, for although mad, he had the gentleness of St. Francis. He helped Hergenhan in our garden on Staten Island, and he liked to walk around in his bare feet. "I can feel things growing," he said. "I look at the little plants, and I'd craw them up out of the earth with the power of love in my eyes."
— Dorothy Day, *The Long Loneliness: An Autobiography*, New York: Harper and Row, 1952, 223

Not all visitors were mad. But many earnest *Catholic Worker* volunteers, visitors and hangers-on could get involved in endless discussions on social, economic or philosophical ideas. I remember Dorothy, walking by unimpressed and muttering instead: "People are ideas!"

"*People* are ideas?" "People *are* ideas?" "People are *ideas?*" What on earth could she mean? Slowly it dawned: Ideas are incarnate in time, in *people*. The world of ideas, their history, their development is a network, woven from people to people, and extending beyond any single person's lifetime.

In one way or another, Dorothy always managed to bring all subjects—war, peace, city, farm, school, factory, exploitation, justice—all back to people living in real time.

Dorothy was not a preacher or talker. She just lived, and she wrote as she lived. But it took time for me to recognize and absorb something of her simple people-minded view. Over the years, the realization became ever clearer.

Houses for Worship

Dorothy had directed my youthful enthusiasm and energies toward the liturgy. A half-century later, in my work with church buildings, I find myself more and more concerned with the practical details of how the people will use the building, will see, hear and move in it, even down to: "How will they change the light bulbs?"

My thoughts about church acoustics, lighting, processions, seating, ambo, baptistry, altar, images, song leader, ushers, vesting room, sacristy, ventilation, safety, flooring, parking, seasons, you name it, are all concerned with people.

Yet, so many churches are, alas, designed only around aesthetic ideas, theological ideas, "contemporary" ideas. How I want to share with architects, building committees and consultants that great phrase of Dorothy's, "People are ideas."

Yes, I am ready to go. After all these decades, I look forward to the angels leading me into paradise. But I will not mind if the Lord gives me a few more years here, more time to work.

That coffin can wait a little longer.

■ *Ade Bethune*

■ EPILOGUE

As Ade Bethune wrote on her coffin: "Life is changed, not ended." The door of death and our experience of time open to eternity. This is a fundamental Christian teaching (see the Second Vatican Council, *Pastoral Constitution on the Church in the Modern World,* 18).

Because we human beings bear in ourselves the seed of eternity, which cannot be reduced to matter alone, we rebel against death. Our minds fail before the mystery of death, but Christian faith reveals that it will be overcome when we recover that wholeness that we lost through sin. For God still calls us to cling to the divine being that we discover through Christ. Faith provides thoughtful people with an answer to those anxious questions about the future.

Eternity Springs from Time

There is something "eternal," that is, something more than simply the "now," more than time, perishing, giving way to something else, changing, replacing. Here are some considerations.

Persistence during Change. The enduring quality of any reality is what persists while sustaining change. Ade remains Ade though the cellular structure of her body has changed many times in her lifetime. When I get married, so many things about me change, but I am still the person I was. (See Stephen Jay Gould, *Time's Arrow, Time's Cycle: Myth and Metaphor in the Discovery of Geological Time*, Cambridge: Harvard University, 1987.)

Combining Past, Present and Future into One. This is an experience of time that goes beyond the clock. In a way, time stands still; it is just "not there" because we have effectively unified past, present and future into one, like Mark Searle's description of the experience expressed in "I could have died and gone to heaven." (See also Thomas Flanagan, *The Tenants of Time*, New York: E. P. Dutton, 1988.)

Liturgy focuses on this unity: "Christ has died; Christ is risen; Christ will come again." In baptism, as I am brought to newness, God summarizes in my life all those works performed to release Israel from bondage and Jesus Christ from death. In confirmation, that is, in my baptismal chrismation, the same Holy Spirit that came down on Jesus in the form of a dove comes down on me, and the same divine voice thunders from the cloud, "This is my beloved child." The source and culmination of the eucharist is the presence in mystery of Christ's saving death and resurrection for us now and the anticipation of the heavenly banquet to come. Anointing of the sick has the purpose not only of physical or emotional healing but the wholeness that befits the reign of God in eternity. Matrimony, according to Ephesians 5:32, mysteriously echoes the relation between Christ who is eternal and the church that is in time; how marvelously marriage offers the experience of eternity! Can there be doubt?

Liturgy's job is to maintain the tension between time and eternity, but this maintenance goes on in private, too. In Luke 5:1–11 there are two scenes: a liturgical scene in which Jesus addresses crowds from a boat about the reign of God, but then Jesus and Simon Peter set out alone to the deep. The lonely deep is where Simon's sacramental call to mission, to become a fisher of people and his sacramental affirmative response take place. The unification of past, present and future takes place in liturgy, in the classroom, in the home, at work and alone in prayer. (See Karl Rahner, *On the Theology of Death*, New York: Herder, 1961; *Theological Investigations*, 18 and 19, New York: Crossroad, 1983.)

Decisions That Stick. Another hint at the existence of eternity is the experience of establishing one's identity with God. This forward step toward becoming one's free self in which time truly creates eternity is experienced in time, like Ade's acceptance of weakness and her growing friendship with her body, but it goes deeper than time and persists beyond time. Nothing takes it away. It sticks. It is a decision with a capital "D." (See Regis Duffy's excellent article, "American Time and God's Time," *Worship*, November, 1988, 515-32.)

At least we cannot say that everything is merely temporal. These experiences permit us to imagine at least something about eternal life:

> Let all the earth stand in awe of God;
>> Let all who dwell in the world revere the Lord.
> For God spoke, and it was made;
>> The Lord commanded, and it came into being.
> The mystery of the Lord stands forever;
>> The design of God's heart through all eternity.
> — *Psalm 33:8–11*

The experience of God's love in our lifetime leaves us in faith and in hope, still waiting for the definitive end without the arrogance of triumph before that end comes. (This arrogance is what Paul rejected in his first letter to the Christians at Corinth; see especially 8:1–13; 10:23–24; 11:17–34.)

Meanwhile, we have Friday fast, Sabbath rest and Sunday celebration, uniting us with the past and with eternity. We have Eastertime, a whole 50 great days of Sunday as though we already live in eternity. (See Robert Taft, "Toward a Theology of the Christian Feast," *Beyond East and West: Problems in Liturgical Understanding*, Washington, D.C.: The Pastoral Press, 1984.)

The Fullness of the Reign of God

So eternity is the experience of God's fullness in us, complete harmony with all life. Then "thy kingdom" truly will have "come." Then "thy will is done." Then God's love will be fully victorious in us. Eternity is assuming ultimate responsibility in obedience to our own conscience, ultimate selfless love and ultimate selfless commitment to truth.

This is the possibility of time and eternity to which all are freely called. Christianity says that time, whenever lived in faith, hope and love, opens to the eternity of supreme happiness, for it has received God and is therefore without end and beyond time.

God's love points to the cross and resurrection of Jesus as its full manifestation:

> Death is swallowed up; victory is won!
> Death, where is your victory?
> O Death, where is your sting?
> — *1 Corinthians 15:55*

This love assures that our brief life span in time ending in death actually creates an eternity that is not made of time but springs from it and goes far beyond. If it seems that death is final, this is because eternity is something we can only faintly imagine but cannot see clearly yet. "Now we see only puzzling reflections in a mirror, but then we shall see face-to-face. My knowledge now is partial; then it will be whole, like God's knowledge of me." (1 Corinthians 13:12)

The city of the reign of God in eternity springs from time and awes us with its goodness:

> Then I saw a new heaven and a new earth. The former heaven and the former earth passed away, and the sea was no more. I also saw the holy city, a new Jerusalem, coming down out of heaven from God, prepared as a bride adorned for her husband. I heard a loud voice from the throne saying, "Behold, God's dwelling is with the human race. The Lord will wipe every tear from their eyes, and there shall be no more death or mourning, wailing or pain, for the old order has passed away. The one who sat on the throne said, "Behold, I make all things new . . . I am the Alpha and the Omega, the beginning and the end."
> — *Revelation 21:1–5*

▪ *James A. Wilde*

■ AUTHORS

John F. Baldovin, SJ, is associate professor of historical and liturgical theology at the Jesuit School of Theology, Berkeley, California. Currently, he is visiting professor of theology at the University of Notre Dame, Notre Dame, Indiana. His works include *The Urban Character of Christian Worship* and several other books and articles.

Ade Bethune of Newport, Rhode Island, was born in 1914 in Schaerbeek, Belgium, near Brussels, came to the United States in 1928, wrote *Work* and illustrated several books for children. Her fame as the illustrator of the *Catholic Worker* for almost 40 years is international. Many of her illustrations are still used in it, and others are available in the collection *Eye Contact.* Her biography, *Proud Donkey of Schaerbeek,* by Judith Staughton, CSJ, is highly recommended.

Andrew D. Ciferni, OPRAEM, is a member of Daylesford Abbey and serves as formation director for the students of his community in Washington. Professor of homiletics and liturgy at the Catholic University of America and adjunct professor of liturgy at the Washington Theological Union, he is adviser to the Bishops' Committee on the Liturgy, member of the advisory board of the Notre Dame Center for Pastoral Liturgy and secretary for the Academy of Preachers.

Lawrence S. Cunningham, formerly professor of religion at Florida State University, currently professor of theology at the University of Notre Dame, is the author of several books, including: *The Catholic Heritage, The Catholic Faith: An Introduction* and *The Catholic Experience.*

Peter Mazar, editor of annual publications for Liturgy Training Publications, authored *Welcome, Yule!, Keeping Advent and Christmastime* and many other books and articles on liturgy, Jewish and Christian customs and plant breeding. He holds a graduate degree in horticultural genetics from Rutgers University.

Gertrud Mueller Nelson is a wife, mother, artist, lecturer and author of *Clip-art for Feasts and Seasons, Clip-art for Celebrations and Service, To Dance with God: Family Ritual and Community Celebration* and numerous articles on liturgy, education, psychology, homemaking and prayer.

Barbara O'Dea, DW, provincial of the Daughters of Wisdom of the American Province, currently serves on the steering committee of the North American Forum on the Catechumenate, was a member of the RCIA subcommittee of the Bishops' Committee on the Liturgy and authored *The Once and Future Church.*

Mary Perkins Ryan, Goffstown, New Hampshire, is a pioneer in religious education and the liturgical movement in the United States. In 1940 she was the first and only woman selected to give a formal address for the First Liturgical Conference meeting. She founded and then served as editor of *Professional Approaches to Christian Education* for 19 years. Among the many books she authored are *Beginning at Home, What is This "Active Participation"?* and *Perspective for Renewal.* We proudly begin our book with a Foreword by Mary.

Mark Searle is associate professor of theology at the University of Notre Dame, coordinator of the Graduate Program in Liturgical Studies and associate director for liturgy in the Notre Dame Study of Catholic Parish Life. His publications include: *Christening: The Making of Christians, Liturgy Made Simple* and many other books and articles. Currently he and his family are on sabbatical in Amsterdam.

James A. Wilde is editor of *Catechumenate: A Journal of Christian Initiation* and the *Font and Table Series* for Liturgy Training Publications. He authored *The Social World of the Gospel of Mark* and coauthored *When Catholics Speak about Jews: Notes for Homilists and Catechists.*

■ APPENDIX

The Liturgical Year

Most of the following information is from *Mysterii paschalis celebrationem,* issued *motu proprio* by Pope Paul VI in 1969, translated as the *Roman Calendar: Text and Commentary* in 1975 by the International Committee on English in Liturgy, adapted, clarified and approved as *Norms Governing Liturgical Calendars* in 1984 by the United States Catholic Conference, Washington D.C.

DAY

The holiness of the liturgical day is manifest in the liturgical celebrations of the people of God, especially the eucharist and the Liturgy of the Hours: Morning Prayer, Daytime Prayer, Evening Prayer, Night Prayer, Office of Readings. The general form for Morning Prayer and Evening Prayer is: Hymn, Psalms, Readings, Responsory, Canticle, Intercessions, Lord's Prayer, Prayer. The lectionaries for the eucharist and Liturgy of the Hours assign readings for these celebrations for each day of the year. The sacramentary is the book of prayers, acclamations and special directions for the celebration of the eucharist each day of the year.

WEEK

Sunday, or the *Lord's Day,* is the celebration of the paschal mystery on the first day of the week. This follows a tradition handed down from the apostles and has its origin on the day of Christ's resurrection. Sunday is the first holy day. *Friday,* a day of penance, recalling the death of Jesus on the cross, is observed by many as a day of penance, charity and prayer.

YEAR: SEASONS

The date of *Easter* determines the most important seasons within the liturgical year. Easter is always on the first Sunday after the first full moon after the vernal equinox. The 40 days of *Lent* immediately precede the Thursday before Easter, beginning on *Ash Wednesday*. Lent is a penitential season of prayer, almsgiving and fasting in preparation for the great paschal mystery, the *Triduum* (Great Three Days) of the passover of Jesus Christ from death on the the cross to the risen glory of Easter. Triduum begins on *Holy Thursday* evening, continues through *Good Friday* and *Holy Saturday* and ends on the evening of Easter. *Eastertime*, a period of the Great 50 Days (seven weeks of seven days, plus one day), ends on *Pentecost. Ascension Thursday* takes place on the 40th day of Eastertime.

Advent and *Christmastime* celebrate the same paschal mystery. The emphasis during these seasons, however, is on the images of light and darkness. Advent is a four-week time of joyful preparation for the coming of Jesus Christ. Christmastime, the celebration of the incarnation of the Second Person of the Trinity, begins with the first Mass on December 25 and comes to a climax on *Epiphany*, the great celebration of God's salvific light for the whole world, manifest in Jesus Christ. After Epiphany, the Baptism of the Lord ends the Christmas season with a similar theophany of light, dove, a voice from the cloud saying, "This is my beloved son, listen to him."

YEAR: ORDINARY TIME

Ordinary Time is time made up of weeks between these seasons. It amounts to about 34 weeks in the yearly cycle. This time is devoted to the mystery of Christ in all its aspects. It begins on the Monday after the Sunday following January 6 and continues until the Tuesday before Lent, that is, Mardi Gras, the day given to carnival before the discipline of penance, charity and prayer begins. Oridnary Time begins again on Monday after Pentecost and ends before evening prayer on the eve of the First Sunday of Advent, when the new church calendar year begins.

Rogation and Ember Days are opportunities to offer prayer to the Lord for the needs of all people, especially for the productivity of the earth and for human labor, and to offer God public thanks.

RANKING DAYS

Solemnities, Feasts, Memorials name the rank of importance the church gives to celebrations of Christ, Mary, martyrs and other saints. Easter and Christmas are, of course, the two greatest solemnities.

SAINTS' DAYS

The *Sanctoral Cycle* has undergone critical revision over the past 20 years regarding ranks, titles, historical considerations, appropriate days, regional or universal appeal. The day a saint is remembered by the church is often, but not always, the day of that saint's death. The day of a saint's death is called the day of that saint's heavenly birthday.

The Roman Calendar

The following is a calendar of all solemnities, feasts and memorials whose dates are fixed. Sundays and the seasons of Advent, Lent and Easter are not fixed. They are "movable feasts" and so do not appear here.

JANUARY

1
SOLEMNITY Mary, Mother of God (Octave of Christmas)
"Theotokos," "God-Bearer," has been the title used for the Blessed Virgin from most ancient times. All the churches recall her memory under this title in their daily eucharistic prayer and especially in the annual celebration of Christmas.

2
MEMORIAL Basil the Great and Gregory Nazianzen, bishops and doctors.
The former died at Caesarea in Cappadocia in 379. The latter died at Nazianzus in 390.

4
MEMORIAL Elizabeth Ann Seton, mother, religious (USA)
founded the Daughters of Charity, died in 1821

5
MEMORIAL John Neumann, bishop (USA)
Redemptorist, bishop of Philadelphia, died in 1860

6
MEMORIAL Blessed Andre Besette, religious (USA)

SOLEMNITY Epiphany of the Lord (Second Sunday after Christmas Day)
(In the USA, this solemnity is on the Sunday after New Year's Day. On the general Roman Calendar, however, it is on January 6.)

FEAST Baptism of the Lord (First Sunday after Epiphany)
(In the USA, if Epiphany is on January 7 or 8, the Baptism is on the very next day.) The final day of Christmastime in which the Father reveals Jesus as the "beloved" child."

7
MEMORIAL Raymond of Penyafort, priest
died in Barcelona in 1275

13
MEMORIAL Hilary, bishop and doctor
died at Poitiers in Gaul, in 367

17
MEMORIAL Anthony, abbot
Jerusalem celebrated Anthony's birthday from the fifth century.

20
MEMORIAL Fabian, pope and martyr
buried in Rome in 250

MEMORIAL Sebastian, martyr
died in Rome in about 300

21
MEMORIAL Agnes, virgin and martyr
buried in Rome in the third century

22
MEMORIAL Vincent, deacon and martyr
buried in Valencia, Spain, in the third century

24
MEMORIAL Francis de Sales, bishop and doctor
died at Lyons in 1622

25
FEAST Conversion of Paul, apostle
See Acts of the Apostles 9:1–30.

26
MEMORIAL Timothy and Titus, bishops
For these disciples of Paul, see Romans 16:21 and Titus 1:4.

27
MEMORIAL Angela Merici, virgin
died in 1540 in Brescia, Italy

28
MEMORIAL Thomas Aquinas, priest and doctor
died near Terracina, Italy, in 1274

31

MEMORIAL John Bosco, priest
died in Turin in 1888

FEBRUARY

2

FEAST Presentation of the Lord
Also called the Purification of Mary and, elsewhere, Candlemas. See Luke 1:22–32; 2:22–40.

3

MEMORIAL Blase, bishop and martyr
The cult of Blase enjoys great popularity in some regions.

MEMORIAL Ansgar, bishop
died in Bremen, Germany, in 865

5

MEMORIAL Agatha, virgin and martyr
died in Sicily in about 250

6

MEMORIAL Paul Miki, priest, and Companions, martyrs
Paul and 25 companions were crucified in Nagasaki, Japan, in 1597.

8

MEMORIAL Jerome Emiliani, priest
died at Somascha, Italy, 1537

10

MEMORIAL Scholastica, virgin
buried at Monte Cassino about 547

11

MEMORIAL Our Lady of Lourdes

14

MEMORIAL Cyril, monk, and Methodius, bishop
They were apostles to Slavic people in the ninth century.

17

MEMORIAL Seven Founders of the Servite Order
14th century

21
MEMORIAL Peter Damian, bishop and doctor
died in Faenza, Italy, in 1072

22
FEAST Chair of Peter, apostle
observed as early as 354

23
MEMORIAL Polycarp, bishop and martyr
martyred at Smyrna in 155

MARCH

3
MEMORIAL Blessed Katharine Drexel (USA)
Whe evangelized African Americans and Native Americans.

4
MEMORIAL Casimir
died at Vilna, Lithuania, in 1484

7
MEMORIAL Perpetua and Felicity, martyrs
died at Carthage in 203

8
MEMORIAL John of God, religious
died at Granada, Spain, in 1550

9
MEMORIAL Frances of Rome, religious
died in 1440

17
MEMORIAL Patrick, bishop
died in Ireland in 461

18
MEMORIAL Cyril of Jerusalem, bishop and doctor
died in Jerusalem in 386

19
SOLEMNITY Joseph, husband of Mary
See Matthew 1:18–25.

23
MEMORIAL Turibius de Mogrovejo, bishop
died at Lima, Peru, in 1606

25
SOLEMNITY Annunciation of the Lord
See Luke 1:26–38.

APRIL

2
MEMORIAL Francis of Paola, hermit
died near Tours, France, in 1507

4
MEMORIAL Isidore, bishop and doctor
died at Seville in 636

5
MEMORIAL Vincent Ferrer, priest
died at Vannes, France, in 1419

7
MEMORIAL John Baptist de la Salle, priest
died at Rouen, France, in 1719

11
MEMORIAL Stanislaus, bishop and martyr
martyred at Cracow, Poland, in 1079

13
MEMORIAL Martin I, pope and martyr
died in the Crimea in 656

21
MEMORIAL Anselm, bishop and doctor
died at Canterbury, England, in 1109

23
MEMORIAL George, martyr
The cult of George seems to have begun in Lydda, Palestine.

24
MEMORIAL Fidelis of Sigmaringen, priest and martyr
martyred at Seewis, Switzerland, in 1622

25
FEAST Mark, evangelist
See Mark 16:15–20.

28
MEMORIAL Peter Chanel, priest and martyr
died on the island of Futuna in the New Hebrides, in 1841

29
MEMORIAL Catherine of Siena, virgin and doctor
She was instrumental in ending the Avignon papacy and died in Rome at age 33 in 1380.

30
MEMORIAL Pius V, pope
died at Rome in 1572

MAY

1
MEMORIAL Joseph the Worker

2
MEMORIAL Athanasius, bishop and doctor
buried at Alexandria, Egypt, in 373

3
FEAST Philip and James, apostles
See Acts of the Apostles 8, John 1:43–40; 6:1–15.

12
MEMORIAL Nereus and Achilleus, martyrs
the martyrs of the Ardeatine Way

MEMORIAL Pancras, martyr
the martyr of the Aurelian Way

14
FEAST Matthias, apostle
See Acts of the Apostles 1:15–26.

15
MEMORIAL Isidore (USA)
died at Seville in 636

18
MEMORIAL John I, pope and martyr
died in prison at Ravenna in 526

20
MEMORIAL Bernardine of Siena, priest
died at Aquila, Italy, in 1444

25
MEMORIAL Venerable Bede, priest and doctor
died at Jarrow, England, in 735

MEMORIAL Gregory VII, pope
died at Salerno, Italy, in 1085

MEMORIAL Mary Magdalene de Pazzi, virgin
died at Florence in 1607

26
MEMORIAL Philip Neri, priest
died at Rome in 1595

27
MEMORIAL Augustine of Canterbury, bishop
died at Canterbury, England, in 605

31
FEAST Visitation
See Luke 1:39–56.

SOLEMNITY Holy Trinity (First Sunday after Pentecost)

SOLEMNITY Body and Blood of Christ (Second Sunday after Pentecost)

SOLEMNITY Sacred Heart (Third Friday after Pentecost)

JUNE

1
MEMORIAL Justin, martyr
died in Rome in about 165

2
MEMORIAL Marcellinus and Peter, martyrs
died in about 304

3
MEMORIAL Charles Lwanga and Companions, martyrs
Charles and 21 companions were martyred at Rubaga, Uganda, in 1886.

5
MEMORIAL Boniface, bishop and martyr
martyred near Dokkum, Holland, in 754

6
MEMORIAL Norbert, bishop
died at Magdeburg, Germany, in 1134

9
MEMORIAL Ephrem, deacon and doctor
died in Edessa in 378

11
MEMORIAL Barnabas, apostle
See Acts of the Apostles 9:26—15:41.

13
MEMORIAL Anthony of Padua, priest and doctor
died in Padua, Italy, in 1231

19
MEMORIAL Romuald, abbot
died near Ravenna in 1027

21
MEMORIAL Aloysius Gonzaga, religious
died at Rome in 1591

22
MEMORIAL Paulinus of Nola, bishop
died in 451

MEMORIAL John Fisher, bishop and martyr, and Thomas More, martyr
John was martyred in London in 1535; Thomas More was martyred in London the same year.

24
SOLEMNITY Birth of John the Baptist,
Luke 1:57–66, 80

27
MEMORIAL Cyril of Alexandria, bishop and doctor
died in 444

28
MEMORIAL Irenaeus, bishop and martyr
died in Lyons, France, in 202

29
SOLEMNITY Peter and Paul, apostles
Peter was crucified in Rome; Paul was beheaded near Rome.

30
MEMORIAL First Martyrs of the Church of Rome
martyred in the Vatican Circus under Nero in 64

JULY

3
FEAST Thomas, apostle
mentioned in John 20:24–29

4
MEMORIAL Elizabeth of Portugal
died at Estremoz, Portugal, in 1336

5
MEMORIAL **Anthony Zaccaria, priest**
died at Cremona, Italy, in 1539

6
MEMORIAL **Maria Goretti, virgin and martyr**
martyred at Nettuno in the Roman Campagna in 1906

11
MEMORIAL **Benedict, abbot**
founder of the Benedictine Order, died at Monte Cassino in 547

13
MEMORIAL **Henry**
died at Bamberg, Germany, in 1024

14
MEMORIAL **Kateri Tekakwitha, virgin (USA)**
Mohawk Indian, died in 1680

MEMORIAL **Camillus de Lellis, priest**
died at Rome in 1614

15
MEMORIAL **Bonaventure, bishop and doctor of the church**
Successor of Francis of Assisi, died at Lyons, France, in 1274

16
MEMORIAL **Our Lady of Mount Carmel**
observance begun by the Carmelites in 1386

21
MEMORIAL **Lawrence of Brindisi, priest and doctor**
died at Lisbon, Portugal, in 1619

22
MEMORIAL **Mary Magdalene**
According to John 20:1–10, Christ first appeared to her.

23
MEMORIAL **Bridget, religious**
died at Rome in 1373

25
FEAST **James, apostle**
martyrdom mentioned in Acts 12:1–2

26
MEMORIAL **Joachim and Ann, parents of Mary**
Joachim means "the Lord will judge;" Ann means "grace."

29
MEMORIAL Martha
She is memtioned in John 11 and elsewhere, with Mary and Lazarus at Bethany.

30
MEMORIAL Peter Chrysologus, bishop and doctor
died in Rome in 451

31
MEMORIAL Ignatius of Loyola, priest
founder of the Jesuit Order, died at Rome in 1556

AUGUST

1
MEMORIAL Alphonsus Ligouri, bishop and doctor
died at Nocera, Italy, in 1787

2
MEMORIAL Eusebius of Vercelli, bishop
died at Vercelli, Italy, in 371

4
MEMORIAL John Vianney, priest
died at Ars, France, in 1859

5
MEMORIAL Dedication of the Church of St. Mary Major
during the pontificate of Sixtus III (432–40)

6
FEAST Transfiguration of the Lord
See Mark 9:2–8; Matthew 17:1–8; Luke 9:28–36.

7
MEMORIAL Sixtus II, pope and martyr, and Companions, martyrs
martyred in 258

MEMORIAL Cajetan, priest
died at Naples in 1547

8
MEMORIAL Dominic, priest
founder of the Dominican Order, died at Bologna in 1221

10
FEAST Lawrence, deacon and martyr
martyred with Sixtus II in Rome in the third century

11
MEMORIAL Clare, virgin
foundress of the Poor Clares, died at Assisi in 1253

13
MEMORIAL Pontian, pope and martyr, and Hippolytus, priest and martyr
martyred in 235 under Maximus

14
MEMORIAL Maximilian Mary Kolbe, priest and martyr
He was a Polish Franciscan martyred at Auschwitz in 1941.

15
SOLEMNITY Assumption
This title and solemnity date to eighth-century Rome.

16
MEMORIAL Stephen of Hungary
died at Szekesfehervar, Hungary, in 1038

18
MEMORIAL Jane Frances de Chantal, religious
died at Molines, France, in 1641

19
MEMORIAL John Eudes, priest
died at Caen, France, in 1680

20
MEMORIAL Bernard, abbot and doctor
died at Clairvaux, France, in 1153

21
MEMORIAL Pius X, pope
died at Rome in 1914

22
MEMORIAL Queenship of Mary
This memorial was established by Pius XII in 1955.

23
MEMORIAL Rose of Lima, virgin
died at Lima, Peru, in 1617

24
FEAST Bartholomew, apostle
mentioned in Mark 3:18, Matthew 10:3 and Luke 6:14

25
MEMORIAL Louis IX
Louis IX, King of France, died near Tunis, North Africa, in 1270

MEMORIAL Joseph Calasanz
died at Rome in 1648

27
MEMORIAL Monica
mother of Augustine of Hippo

28
MEMORIAL Augustine, bishop and doctor
died at Hippo, North Africa, in 430

29
MEMORIAL Beheading of John the Baptist
See Mark 1:7–8; 6:17–29.

SEPTEMBER

3
MEMORIAL Gregory the Great, pope and doctor
died at Rome in 604

8
FEAST Birth of Mary
This feast dates to the end of the 5th century.

9
MEMORIAL Peter Claver, priest, missionary (USA)
died in Colombia, South America, in 1654

13
MEMORIAL John Chrysostom, bishop and doctor
died at Comana, in Pontus, in 407

14
FEAST Triumph of the Cross
Veneration of the wood of the cross dates to the fifth century in Jerusalem.

15
MEMORIAL Our Lady of Sorrows
This title and observance began with the Servites in 1667.

16
MEMORIAL Cornelius, pope and martyr, and Cyprian, bishop and martyr
Cornelius died at Civitavecchia, Italy, in 253; Cyprian died at Carthage in 258.

17
MEMORIAL Robert Bellarmine, bishop and doctor
died at Rome in 1621

19
MEMORIAL Januarius, bishop and martyr
died at Puteoli, near Naples, in 305 under Diocletian

21
FEAST Matthew, apostle and evangelist
See Matthew 9:9–13.

26
MEMORIAL Cosmas and Damian, martyrs
martyred around 305 under Diocletian

27
MEMORIAL Vincent de Paul, priest
died at Paris in 1660

28
MEMORIAL Wenceslaus, martyr
died at Boleslavia, Bohemia, in 929

29
FEAST Michael, Raphael and Gabriel, archangels
See Tobit 12:15; Daniel 8:15, 9:21; Luke 1:11–20, 6–38.

30
MEMORIAL Jerome, priest and doctor
buried at Bethlehem in 420

OCTOBER

1
MEMORIAL Theresa of the Child Jesus, virgin
died at Lisieux, France, in 1897

2
MEMORIAL Guardian Angels
See Psalms 103:20; 138:1.

4
MEMORIAL Francis of Assisi
died at Assisi in 1226

6

MEMORIAL Blessed Marie-Rose Durocher, virgin (USA)
new to the national calendar

MEMORIAL Bruno, priest
died at La Torre, Italy, in 1101

7

MEMORIAL Our Lady of the Rosary
The memorial was instituted in 1573 after the Christian victory at Lepanto.

9

MEMORIAL Denis, bishop and martyr, and Companions, martyrs
See Acts 17:13–34, died in Gaul, near today's Paris.

MEMORIAL John Leonardi, priest
John, who founded the Clerks Regular of the Mother of God, died at Rome in 1609.

14

MEMORIAL Callistus I, pope and martyr
died at Rome in 222

15

MEMORIAL Teresa of Jesus (of Avila), virgin and doctor
died at Alba de Tormes, Spain, in 1582

16

MEMORIAL Hedwig, religious
died at Trebnitz, Poland, in 1243

MEMORIAL Margaret Mary Alacoque, virgin
died at Paray-l-Monial, France, in 1690

17

MEMORIAL Ignatius of Antioch, bishop and martyr
martyred at Rome about 107

18

FEAST Luke, evangelist
In Colossians 4:14, he is called the "beloved physician."

19

MEMORIAL Isaac Jogues and John de Brebeuf, priests and martyrs, and Companions, martyrs (USA)
Isaac, John and John de Lande, layperson, died near Auriesville, New York, in 1647

MEMORIAL Paul of the Cross, priest
died at Rome in 1775

23
MEMORIAL John of Capistrano, priest
died at Villach, Austria, in 1456

24
MEMORIAL Anthony Mary Claret, bishop
died near Narbonne, France, in 1870

28
FEAST Simon and Jude, apostles
Luke 6:12–16

NOVEMBER

1
SOLEMNITY All Saints
Rome adopted this solemnity in the ninth century.

2
All Souls
Instituted by Odilo at Cluny in 998; by Rome in 1300

3
MEMORIAL Martin de Porres, religious
died at Lima, Peru, in 1639

4
MEMORIAL Charles Borromeo, bishop
died at Milan in 1584

9
FEAST Dedication of St. John Lateran
Constantine's basilica was built around 324.

10
MEMORIAL Leo the Great, pope and doctor
died in 461

11
MEMORIAL Martin of Tours, bishop
died at Tours, France, in 397

12
MEMORIAL Josaphat, bishop and martyr
martyred at Vitepsk, Russia, in 1623

13

MEMORIAL Frances Xavier Cabrini, virgin (USA)
She was born in Italy in 1850, immigrated to the U.S. in 1889 and died of malaria in Chicago in 1917.

15

MEMORIAL Albert the Great, bishop and doctor
died at Cologne in 1280

16

MEMORIAL Margaret of Scotland
died at Edinburgh in 1093

MEMORIAL Gertrude, virgin
died near Eisleben, Germany, in 1302

17

MEMORIAL Elizabeth of Hungary, religious
died at Marburg, Germany, in 1231

18

MEMORIAL Dedication of the Churches of Peter and Paul
in the 11th century at Rome

MEMORIAL Rose Philippine Duchesne (USA)

21

MEMORIAL Presentation of Mary
This observance originated at Jerusalem in 543.

22

MEMORIAL Cecilia, virgin and martyr
There has been a church in her honor at Rome since 313.

23

MEMORIAL Clement I, pope and martyr
the fourth pope, died in about 101

MEMORIAL Columban, abbot
died at Bobbio, Italy, in 615

30

FEAST Andrew, apostle
See Mark 1:16–29; 13:1–4.

SOLEMNITY Christ the King (Last Sunday in Ordinary Time)

DECEMBER

3
MEMORIAL Francis Xavier, priest
died in China in 1552

4
MEMORIAL John of Damascus, priest and doctor
died near Jerusalem in 749

6
MEMORIAL Nicholas, bishop
died at Myra, in Lycia (Turkey), in the fourth century

7
MEMORIAL Ambrose, bishop and doctor
died at Milan, Italy, in 397

8
SOLEMNITY Immaculate Conception of Mary
Patron of the USA. This solemnity has been observed since 1476 at Rome.

11
MEMORIAL Damasus I, pope
died at Rome in 384

12
FEAST Our Lady of Guadalupe (USA)
Patron of the Americas. This feast recalls the events of 1531 when Mary appeared to a Mexican Indian named Juan Diego.

13
MEMORIAL Lucy, virgin and martyr
martyred at Syracuse, Sicily, in 305 under Diocletian

14
MEMORIAL John of the Cross, priest and doctor
died at Ubeda, Spain, in 1591

21
MEMORIAL Peter Canisius, priest and doctor
died at Fribourg, Switzerland, in 1587

23
MEMORIAL John of Kanty, priest
died at Cracow, Poland, in 1473

25

SOLEMNITY **Christmas**

The yearly observance was instituted at Rome about 330 with Mass around 9:00 AM; inspired by the Christian observance of Epiphany in Jerusalem, the Mass at midnight was added in the Basilica of St. Mary Major in the fifth century, with Lauds afterward; around the middle of the sixth century a third Mass was added in the church of St. Anastasia near the Palatine at which the pope presided. The three are called: Midnight Mass, Mass at Dawn, Mass during the Day.

26

FEAST **Stephen, first martyr**

See Acts of the Apostles 6 and 7.

27

FEAST **John, apostle and evangelist**

See the Gospel of John and Acts 4:19–20.

28

FEAST **Holy Innocents, martyrs**

See Matthew 2:1–18 and Exodus 1:15–22.

29

MEMORIAL **Thomas Becket, bishop and martyr**

martyred at Canterbury, England, in 1170

31

MEMORIAL **Sylvester I, pope**

died in Rome in 335

FEAST **Holy Family (The Sunday after Christmas Day)**

(When Christmas Day itself is a Sunday, this feast is kept on December 30.)